Master Change or it will
Master You!

[handwritten signature]

THE REALITY OF CHANGE

Dr. Fred Johnson and
Dr. Paul Metler

The Reality of Change

Dr. Fred Johnson and
Dr. Paul Metler

Book Two
Rising Tide Leadership Series
The Reality of Change

http://www.Initiative-One.com

Published by:
9th Street Publishing
www.9thstreetpublishing.com

ISBN: 978-0-982-10507-8
Printed in the United States of America
First Edition © 2015

TABLE OF CONTENTS

FOREWORD

Dr. Fred's teachings and The *Reality of Change* are the definitive guide for individuals and leaders to transform change from a fear-based reaction to a systematic process and powerful ally. The teachings in this book should be required reading for all of us and will improve your leadership skills and overall happiness. For years I struggled with my own internal conflict and a common theme for many of us; believing that I had potential for greater achievements in my personal and professional life, yet not doing anything about it, giving into my fears and self-doubt and not living my dreams. It was not until Dr. Fred's teachings and *The Reality of Change* became a part of my personal development that I was able to overcome these obstacles and begin to view change as a predictable process. Through numerous major career transitions from clinical physician, physician executive, entrepreneur, and corporate executive, the practice of these principles has allowed me to live intentionally, made crossing the line of commitment a less scary process, kept me going in uncertain waters, and led to incredible experiences and results. So begin reading, get going and keep rowing.

Alan Roga, MD
Physician Executive and Entrepreneur

INTRODUCTION

The Island That Would Not Change

My company owns a retreat home nestled on a beautiful island in the middle of one of the Great Lakes. Our stays on the island feel like stepping back in time to a more tranquil, slower, peaceful era absent of the frantic pace of modern American life.

For decades, the residents have deliberately protected the pristine aura of the island. They have been determined to push away attempts to transform it into a bustling, commercial tourist haven. Most of the long-timers have fiercely protected the island against any perceived threat to the status quo. Consequently, the word "change" isn't a pleasant term for them. Resistance to change has been a badge of honor worn proudly by the locals. But the very quality once considered the residents' greatest strength has begun to jeopardize the future of their beloved community's sustainability.

Storms of Protest on the Island

The local history is replete with examples of resistance to change. Just a few years ago the island residents blocked efforts to replace two grass landing strips with modern concrete runways, despite having federal funds in hand. Access to the island is restricted to boats and a single ferry. They feared the new runways would attract "jet set" types—people who would spike real estate prices, build large homes, and cause property tax values to skyrocket. The islanders successfully turned away the project.

Soon after the runway project was thwarted, another storm of protest arose. This time, it was over a new building. The completion of a community performing arts center on the island triggered an emotional reaction. It was funded entirely by a "summer person" who, they claim, "didn't have the right to have a say in our community plans." One old-timer stated crassly, "We don't want this to become a place for the artsy-fartsy. We're just fishing folks."

The divide between full-time natives and part-time residents is not surprising. Beyond the disdain and labels, an attitude of overt hostility toward the influence of "wealthy outsiders" surfaced. In effect, the islanders wanted the outsiders' money but not their ideas. In response to the negativity, newcomers or part-time residents grew increasingly more hesitant to invest in the island economy. They held back lending their expertise to buy or improve businesses. Frequently, they withheld their support of endeavors that would enhance the quality of life for the islanders.

INTRODUCTION

Struggling with a stagnant tax base, the island's main town could not afford to invest in its infrastructure, maintain the quality of school operations, or spend money on strengthening its tourism. The island itself assumed a tired, neglected appearance that dampened its appeal to tourists. Many businesses did not have the necessary capital to keep their locations attractive and up-to-date. As an example, the once-elegant historic hotel with its five-star restaurant was abandoned.

In recent years, jobs became increasingly more scarce. Young adults were forced to leave the island to search for employment. The school's student population diminished, forcing layoffs for teachers. "For Sale" signs dotted the landscape all over the island. New construction ground to a halt. An outsider arriving on the island would witness a struggling community caught in a downward spiral of exodus and decline. The islanders had to face the timeless truth of change: Either we grow or go, move forward or decline. The status quo is not a viable option.

The Island Way

Custom home construction was a longtime staple of the local economy. For decades, homebuilders fueled the island economy. In time, the builders became victims of their own success. They believed they had a closed, captive market—and were quick to inform prospective homeowners about the so-called "island way" of doing things. If you wanted a vacation home or primary residence built, you were forced to accept the fact that builders on the island operated differently than those on the mainland. They said, "We build on island time. We charge island prices. We use island ways." Of course, the "island way" was not particularly customer friendly. The builders were unapologetic about higher costs, delayed completion, and fewer choices for clients.

THE REALITY OF CHANGE

People came to expect the cost of building their homes would exceed mainland pricing by 20 to 30 percent. Added to that, many waited months beyond the agreed-upon start date before an island contractor would commence work. When one contractor was asked why the builders didn't make customer service a priority, he replied, "Because we don't have to."

Storm Damage to the Island Economy

The contractors' attempt to resist change and control the economy was shortsighted, myopic, and selfish.

And the builders were not alone. Other island residents also incorrectly believed their isolation exempted them from experiencing change. Rather than striving to manage and provide benefit to the island, they dug in their heels.

Interestingly, one business owner and community leader shared his observations with me. John is a member of one of the leading families on the island. After a short conversation with him, I was convinced he realized what was happening to his beloved island home. When he shared his thoughts, he almost seemed dejected. John's tone was drenched with sadness and a quiet resignation.

When I asked why he hadn't done more to correct the negative cycle, John sighed. It's not that John hadn't tried. But every time he attempted to move the conversation forward, he met with staunch resistance. Eventually, the resistance turned to ridicule. Members of John's family got the best of him. They begged him to leave well enough alone, afraid that if people got too upset, they would boycott the family business. In the end, John concluded it just wasn't worth it. He learned to stay quiet and not rock the boat. Whether John rocked the boat or not, it was taking on water. Resignation is not a solution.

But despite their staunch refusal to adapt, the island began to shift and their grip on the economy slipped beyond their control. The "island way" was changing without the residents' permission. No island, literally or figuratively, could avoid the inevitable march of change.

Unstoppable Force

Is change always an enemy? Is resistance to it your immediate response? Perspective matters. As long as change was deemed the enemy, it galvanized the perspective of the islanders. By focusing on change as a common foe to be defeated, this island community couldn't see any opportunities objectively. They hastily dismissed positive changes as threats. Any future vision of the island was distorted by fear.

But none of their efforts or fears prevented changes from happening, and the islanders found themselves being dragged along by its unbridled impact. After all, attempting to eliminate all change is like grasping the wind.

If attempts to control or resist change are so unproductive, then why was the island mindset so prevalent? This book examines the allure of the status quo, the emotional forces that persuade you to retreat, and how resistance to change comes from all sides.

Find Yourself in the Story

Did the island story resonate with any of your own experiences? If so, you will benefit from reading this book, *The Reality of Change.* Change is ubiquitous; there's no escaping it. In fact, it can feel like change is encroaching on every area of life. Remaining stuck in status quo mode only ensures you won't be ready to discern the best paths for your life. Mastering positive change leads to reducing your stress and anxiety. The benefits will ripple through both your personal and professional life, and doors to extraordinary leadership and optimal business outcomes will open.

Yes, you *can* learn to embrace change as a pivotal leadership quality. You *can* gain confidence in leading yourself and others into a promising future. You'll also discover positive developments along the way. They supply the will and energy to keep moving forward when everything inside you screams that you should quit and turn around.

Change begins with you. *The Reality of Change* will help you embrace its power for positive change.

Better at Change, Better You, Better Life

Mastering positive change involves navigating emotionally shallow waters and relationship collisions. That includes resistance from within and without, blame, victimhood, false barriers, and other change-busters. As you continue to read, you'll learn to overcome the inner and outer obstacles. You'll also discover how to steer yourself and your organization through the positive change process.

The ability to embrace positive change foreshadows the magnificent benefits you can gain. While not all change leads to positive results, there's no such thing as obtaining *new* positive results without change. Conversely, the inability to accept the inevitable, unstoppable force of change will lead to devastating consequences sooner or later—as the isolated islanders found out. This is one of the undeniable principles of life.

What the Reality of Change Means

In the pages ahead, you'll learn about the predictable behaviors of others, their motives, and their methods as you lead change—whether you are leading yourself or leading others.

If you are about to introduce a new approach to your company or with your team, you will experience The Reality of Change itself. If you are attempting to recreate the culture of a company or address "the sacred cow issues" that are dragging down the organization, this book is for you. If you are committed to creating healthy accountability in your firm, continue reading. If you are about to end a central relationship, start a central relationship, lose twenty pounds, quit your smoking habit, confront a powerful addiction, pursue a longstanding dream, embark on a new career, you will travel this journey. The list of applications is endless.

The Reality of Change touches all aspects of life. It affects businesses, organizations, and religious establishments. Your ability to have an impact, live a meaningful life, and achieve successful outcomes depends on how you handle The Reality of Change.

There is a predictable, observable pattern that accompanies the undertaking of any significant change. Resistance is inevitable and when it's directed at you, it can sting a little. But when you learn to anticipate the pushback, you can overcome the temptation to personalize any opposition you get. Always remember that the pushback against the changes you champion is not personal.

A Transformative Effect

What would happen if you transformed your view on change? What if you learned how to master positive change and lead others through the process? The effect of this transformation will surprise you. Your ability to embrace and engage in meaningful change will extend into all areas of life. Becoming better at change will lead to a better you, a better life.

By following the ideas in this book, you'll discover how to:

- Gain confidence in leading change through knowing what's to come.

- Reduce stress and anxiety in your life.
- Embrace change as a pivotal leadership quality.
- Counter naysaying as you avoid blame and taking things personally.
- Master change in the context of other key leadership traits.
- Successfully guide your organization into new and promising waters.

Yes, it becomes easier to embrace the challenges of being a change agent when you understand it's simply part of a process. Remember, you're not the first person to encounter The Reality of Change, and you won't be the last.

Sir Isaac Newton taught us that for every action there is an equal and opposite reaction. Therefore, the challenges that accompany change should not be unexpected, for similar challenges accompany all significant change initiatives.

In the arena of leadership, for example, if you're committed to leading bold change, then prepare yourself for bold resistance. Know that the greater the change, the greater the resistance will be. Your commitment to be an effective change agent requires you to expect opposition as part of the process. Because deep change awakens deep opposition, you'll need guidance and reassurance that it's possible. Know that real change is worth the price tag.

Launching Your Change Journey

Think of change as a voyage that begins with a launch and a destination in mind. Many factors contribute to your decision to launch. No doubt, you're considering making changes in your life today as you calculate the costs and estimate the rewards. Some outlays are known and many are hidden. Some benefits are obvious and many are obscure. But once you seriously entertain the possibility of a different future, you've entered into The Reality of Change.

What to Expect in This Book

Part I in this book addresses your starting point and prepares you to launch into successful change. Once you seriously consider it, you must begin with acknowledging your current mental and emotional residence. You are Living on the Shore of the Status Quo. And this shoreline can be a miserable place.

As you begin to contemplate positive change, you can expect to experience an uncomfortable tension. You either decide to stay on the shore or break free. If you choose the shore, you will experience a quiet sense of resignation. On the other hand, leaving The Land of Status Quo involves several intentional movements that signal a genuine departure. Your exodus from The Land of Status Quo indicates an internal acceptance of The Price of Crossing the Shoreline.

Part II prepares you for what you will experience next. Once you have crossed the line, your actual journey begins. The Reality of Change mostly occurs between when you launch and when you reach your destination. Don't expect smooth sailing. Before you leave the harbor, you must confront your fears. The wind and waves are real, and voices from the shore will tempt you to return.

Staying the Course on Stormy Seas is easier when you understand how to navigate the challenges. Perhaps Unwanted Stowaways are the greatest threat to your journey, and though their voices beckon from the shore, their messages sneak aboard by finding their way into your head. And, in contrast to the noise of naysayers and doubters, portions of your journey will be filled with deafening silence when you long for an encouraging word. Maintaining momentum through these challenges is the unheralded secret of change. Sometimes the determining factor in a successful change initiative is whether or not you can Keep the Rowers Rowing.

Part III provides the rationale for your investment in change. The launch is critical and the journey transformational in itself, but never underestimate the importance of The Destination. The greater your affinity for the destination, the more you'll be able to tap into The Power of a Clear Purpose. Your purpose for change provides the fuel for your journey. Being clear about your purpose will enable you to recognize the new shoreline on the horizon when you catch a glimpse of The Land of Positive Results.

As you set foot in the new world, you will reap the benefits of the journey. Your arrival provides a unique vantage point, allowing you to see beyond the present with greater passion and clarity. The results you achieve will open pathways to greater challenges and successes in your future that you can't see until you arrive. And these pathways that create your leadership legacy will take you through The Reality of Change.

Journey on!

THE REALITY OF CHANGE		
PART ONE *The Land of Status Quo*	**PART TWO** *Staying the Course on Stormy Seas*	**PART THREE** *The Destination*
Living on the Shore of Status Quo	Unwanted Stowaways	The Power of a Clear Purpose
Leaving the Land of Status Quo	No Attaboy Territory - Resist the Undertow	The Land of Positive Results
The Price of Crossing the Shoreline	Keep the Rowers Rowing	Beware the New Land of Status Quo

The Line of Commitment

THE REALITY OF CHANGE

PART ONE:
THE LAND OF STATUS QUO

"We cannot become what we need to be by remaining what we are."

-Max De Pree

THE REALITY OF CHANGE

CHAPTER ONE

LIVING ON THE SHORE
OF STATUS QUO

"Things changed, people changed, and the world went
rolling along right outside the window."

-Nicholas Sparks

THE REALITY OF CHANGE

A Walk Along the Shore

Stand on a beach. Walk along the shore. Whether you gaze out at the magnificence of an ocean or the beauty of a lake, you experience an unavoidable attraction. It's nearly impossible to stand on the shore and avoid shifting your focus to the deep. For some, a simple glance toward the horizon is inspiring. For others, the shoreline can be a miserable place. The sea can beckon for adventure or represent a fearsome unknown. Similarly, as you begin to contemplate positive change in your life, you'll experience an uncomfortable tension. It's The Reality of Change that begins within you. Your choice is to stay on the shore or break free.

Simply stated, the shore is where you are right now. It's either the beginning of change or the continuation of the status quo.

Be forewarned; a walk on the beach can be disturbing. Once you have elevated your gaze—once you've allowed the salt air to infect your dreams or imagined the wind filling your sails—life on the shore can never be the same. A decision to change opens the door to adventure; a decision to stay on the shore is a form of resignation.

Change is fueled by a belief in what's possible. Fear of change is kept alive by beliefs as well. Have you come to believe certain messages about change that are simply not true? Let's examine Nancy's experience.

Nancy Lives on the Shore

Nancy's resume was impressive. As an attorney, she had a remarkable list of clients, and her early career was the envy of most aspiring young law students. Talented, personable, and highly effective, Nancy possessed the stellar traits of a good attorney. A critical thinker who enjoyed research, she was meticulous in her appearance. Yet, when she walked into our counseling office, she did not exhibit the signs of success. Her outward appearance could not camouflage what was happening on the inside. It didn't require the discernment of a trained counselor to detect her unhappiness. Her eyes were drenched with sadness, and her voice fluctuated between anger and despair.

Nancy felt miserable and needed to tell someone her story. It began with a significant transition. Several years earlier, she had left a position with a powerful law firm and moved from a bustling metropolis to a small Midwestern community in support of her husband Raymond's political pursuits within his hometown's local government. Life in the big city had been busy, productive, and fulfilling. Just describing her former venue brought back a spark in her eye and a shift in her tone and posture. But that was then.

Equally recognizable was the change in Nancy's demeanor when she described her current situation. Despite her initial optimism, the move had not been positive. Being an African American woman in a rural, mostly white community was replete with challenges. Most days, she felt isolated and ostracized. Complaining she was unable to find a professional position appropriate for her knowledge and experience, she felt like an urban professional stuck in the middle of nowhere.

After describing her situation, Nancy quickly moved to her verdict: her husband was guilty for putting her there. In addition, she derided the residents for being so racist. She belittled the business community for having nothing to offer. She declared people in the town shortsighted and devoid of vision. Despite pronouncing guilt on everyone else, Nancy claimed she bore the brunt of the sentence. Feeling stuck with no options, her small town might just as well have been a prison.

Come to find out, this wasn't the first time Nancy shared her story. This angry, resentful lady sang the same song over and over again to herself and others. Sadly, Nancy chose to remain stuck in The Land of Status Quo.

Bob Lives on the Shore

Bob was mired in The Land of Status Quo as well. As the leader of a substantial healthcare division within its parent company, Bob had experienced withering criticism from within the organization for several months. His organization was paralyzed by dissension and infighting among its leaders.

Despite a detailed report from a consultant that revealed steeply declining effectiveness and growing problems throughout the organization, Bob couldn't lift the division out of a deepening crisis. Clearly, he had lost the confidence of his leadership team.

When confronted with the facts, Bob placed blame for his ineffectiveness on organizational politics. When told he needed to make deep changes in his management approach, he resisted. Instead, he diverted attention away from the present crisis toward accolades from the past. For example, Bob would proudly point out various leadership certificates as proof of his vast knowledge and experience. Clearly, he felt under-appreciated.

Bob was quick to communicate his misfortune and the rationale for his perspective. He declared his division was in crisis when he arrived; he inherited a mess; there was nothing he could do to change it. He had concluded his situation was hopeless and daily misery was simply part of the job. Refusing to change, Bob chose to remain on the shore.

CHAPTER ONE

The Land of Quiet Misery

Choosing to remain on The Shore of Status Quo consistently yields a life of quiet misery. It represents those areas you find unsatisfying, unfulfilling, and yet you've chosen to settle there. In the shadow of the trees near the shore lies a private cemetery—a place where dreams are buried and hope is laid to rest. You don't want to visit it often, but you know it's there.

Everyone has areas in life that have been mesmerized by the cozy appeal of the status quo. This transfixed state begins with a reasonable consideration of options and leads to an exchange. When you find yourself accepting a reality in your life that's far less satisfying than you would have chosen in an earlier time, you have settled in The Land of Status Quo. Its symptoms include the following:

- You were once physically fit, but now you wrestle with being forty pounds overweight. You suppress a deep disappointment and shame because you have let yourself go. After a number of diets and ill-fated attempts to regain wellness, you have reached a place of resignation.
- You are feeling oppressed by an unfulfilling job. You long to go back to school to prepare for a new career, but instead you convince yourself you are trapped. You focus on the facts that support your conclusion. Your family needs income. You have too many years invested in your profession. You don't have the time to do it all.
- You are in an abusive relationship. You feel as though you are being robbed of joy and self-worth, but you're afraid to share your plight with friends or family. What will happen if your abuser discovers you have revealed the truth? You have convinced yourself

that life could be worse. Every day you repeat this same message: "Pull yourself together and accept it."

- You are an executive who's worried about the declining results in your company. You know big changes are needed, but you refuse to have an honest conversation with your boss for fear of his reaction. You constantly remind yourself that retirement is only a few years away. You think: "Why stir up anything?"

Hundreds of scenarios illustrate this same message: *Living on The Shore of Status Quo can become a place of resignation.* So why would you choose to dwell there? When did you cease being an explorer and become a settler?

It begins with fear.

Living with Fear

People who choose Living on the Shore of Status Quo have something in common. They all carry with them an internal message of fear. Fear lurks beneath the surface of a choice to live with the status quo despite compelling reasons for change. But remaining complacent or stretching toward new discoveries will largely depend on how you feel about change. Fundamentally, decisions about change begin at an emotional level.

To recognize if you're stuck on the shore requires being mindful of your fears. But behaving with mindfulness isn't as easy as it sounds. Feelings are easily camouflaged. Ask yourself these questions: Have you ever dressed up your fears as carefulness? When confronted with the need to change, how quickly do you make favorable self-comparisons with others who have mistakenly thrown caution to the wind? Are you adept at making a list of serious potential consequences and then undergirding your indecision with the list?

Becoming aware of your answers will help you cut through the facade and admit your fears.

Face it. No matter how you dress it up, you let fear be a constant companion of Living on the Shore of Status Quo. The pseudo-stability of resistance to change is convenient. It can make perfect sense to live in a familiar place. In fact, you believe resisting negative change is a virtue. Your ability to say "no" to negative change rests on your character and convictions, but your resistance to positive change feeds off your fears. For example, your fear of the unknown persuades you to stick with a miserable job or tolerate an abusive relationship.

Have you given into fear and pursued safety rather than meaning? Are you chasing after certainty instead of exhilaration?

Dealing with Your Fears

Fear has many sources including these:

- A fear of discomfort
- A fear of failure
- A fear of disappointment
- A fear of the unknown
- A fear that you are not enough

Know this: Being afraid is not a state of weakness. A person who knows no fear is likely someone who makes horrific impulsive decisions because there's no pause to carefully evaluate before moving forward. But you're dealing with a different kind of fear—the fear of change.

Understand that positive change does not require the absence of fear, but embracing it calls for increasing your self-awareness and asking questions. *Why are you afraid? What fears are driving your behaviors?*

THE REALITY OF CHANGE

Effective people are in touch with their own fears most of the time. They don't ignore them or pretend they have none. Rather, they face them straight on, allowing them to be a catalyst for reflection, preparation, and careful execution. Feeling afraid informs them, but it does not own them. As they process through their fears, they allow their principles, self-belief, and clear pictures of a desired future move them forward with action. They have chosen to live *with* fear rather than live *in* fear.

On the other hand, people mired in The Land of Status Quo have allowed fear to serve as master over their own choices. Living in The Land of Status Quo results from choosing safety over greatness, settling for certainty instead of grasping potential.

Have you chosen to accept a level of mediocrity in any area of your life? Have you silenced your soul? After all, every soul longs for passion, depth, and the refreshing sensation of being truly alive. Yet status quo is a place where people have settled, afraid to feel the discomfort that always accompanies growth and fresh ways.

Life is filled with choices and exchanges. If you exchange your dreams for Living on the Shore of Status Quo, you choose to trade unmet potential for short-term relief from the tension. But the relief doesn't last. Before long, the comfortable shore becomes more tenuous.

At first, the cost of Living on the Shore of Status Quo seems low. A closer inspection of the price reveals hidden costs that measure the price of exchange. Fulfillment is exchanged for predictability, avoiding the unknown. When you choose predictability instead of exhilaration, you risk a loss of fulfillment and self-respect in an effort to preserve a manageable level of comfort. Ultimately, you have to find a way to resolve the tension that results.

CHAPTER ONE

Dealing with Tension and Rationalization

When you are standing on the shore considering a significant change in your life, what happens on the inside? You feel tension—a tension between your dreams and your fears, between the known and the unknown. You don't want to admit it, but you'd rather embrace the terra firma on the shore than experience the challenges of finding your sea legs. This was true for both Bob and Nancy in the earlier examples.

But the tension continues. How do you resolve the tension from the shore? By developing a way to cope with disappointment that gnaws at your gut like a hunger pang. Yet living this way isn't as difficult as it sounds. Here's why.

Human beings have a tremendous capacity to develop coping mechanisms. Since theories about cognitive dissonance burst on the scene several decades ago, many applications have emerged. These theories coalesce into a simple fact: *You learn to cope because dissonance is uncomfortable.*

Some methods of coping are healthy and some are not. Ask this question: If you choose to remain Living on the Shore of Status Quo, what kind of thinking will ease the tension? A common answer is to rationalize your behavior. For example, a woman who died at age 90 had smoked most of her life and rationalized it by saying,

- "They haven't proven that smoking causes cancer."
- "You only live once, so I'm going to do what comforts me."
- "I have to have it for weight loss. Besides, I'm healthier when I'm thinner."
- "Without smoking, I become a nervous wreck. It's better for my peace of mind."
- "I only smoke outside. It's not hurting anyone else, so what's the problem?"

For her, these points justified her living in the realm of status quo. When someone is afraid of change, it becomes easy to justify staying the same.

Beware of Victim Thinking

Once you begin to rationalize, it's easy to slide into a more sinister coping mechanism called victimhood. Said another way, Living on the Shore of Status Quo can lead you to conclude you are a victim. (As a side note, it's important to acknowledge that true victims exist. This advice doesn't attempt to minimize an innocent victim of physical and mental abuse or of violent crimes. Rather, it refers to avoiding the easy route and attributing where you are to sources beyond your control.)

Do you feel stuck Living on the Shore of Status Quo? If so, it's possible you've been tempted to find a measure of self-respect by believing "it's not my fault." Right now, take a moment to fill in the blank in this sentence with your favorite excuse: *I am where I am because* _____. Now pay close attention to the words you filled in. When you think like a victim, you give away your power to those things. As a result, your power to choose to pursue a better future diminishes. And the power of the things or people in life that you blame becomes greater. Your "thought life" becomes plagued by a series of "If only" statements. Here are some examples:

- "I'm not happy because of my job. If only I could have a different job, I would be happy."
- "I'm not productive because of my boss. If only I had a different boss, I would be more productive."
- "I'm not content because of my pay grade. If only I was paid more money, I would be content."
- "I'm not successful because of my spouse. If only I had a different spouse, I would be successful."

In each case, a sense of inner contentment and fulfillment depends on someone or something external. This implies your life is beyond *your* control. Therefore, it's important to recognize these internal messages are your way to cope with tension. Remember, Living on the Shore of Status Quo addresses your way of thinking, and victimhood reflects broken thinking.

As an example, Nate is a highly skilled contractor and young business owner. When he arrived at our house to talk, it was clear he was irritated about something. A simple question about his day opened a floodgate of vitriol. Nate seized this opportunity to vent and rapid-fire frustration spewed out. "I'm so tired of being everybody's grunt. I'm sick of being under-appreciated and underpaid," Nate complained. "My customers tell me that twenty-five dollars an hour is outrageous. I'm angry that I can't pay myself more because my customers will get mad if I do! I'm ready to quit. I'm tired of owning my own business. I'll get away from this mess."

- Nate's anger? Not his fault.
- Nate's frustration? Not his fault.
- Nate's future in business? Not his choice.

Yet Nate's frustration was palpable. And he didn't hide his attitude. Feeling trapped, in his mind there was nothing left to do but give up.

Clearly, Nate's biggest problem was Nate himself. No matter where he chose to work, his biggest problem would be coming with him. More than a job change, he needed a shift in thinking because he was choosing misery. Without even realizing it, he'd grown dependent on the attitude or personality of customers to determine if he'd have a good day.

At a deeper level, Nate had allowed his self-worth to be determined by the person he was working for at the moment. It's a strange paradox. How could such misery become a coping mechanism to ease tension? So becoming a victim feels like a relief because it relieves people of taking "responsibility" for their situation. As Nate showed, people can derive a strange comfort from convincing themselves their life situation is out of their control.

Dealing with Victim Thinking

How can you escape victim thinking? With truth. The truth is you do not control what happens to you. Acknowledging this is the first step. And the truth is you do control what happens inside you when something happens to you!

Know this: You are a steward of all the opportunities and unique qualities you have received. You were fashioned to reach your highest potential. No one else can be responsible for the choices that will propel you toward a life of purpose and fulfillment. Will you be an effective, efficient steward of the attributes you have been given? Will you choose to be the best possible version of you? When you make the proper choices, you are being authentic and true to your identity. It's impossible to put a price tag on your identity.

By accepting your intrinsic value as a unique creation, you embrace the meaning, impact, and joy you're meant to experience. Life is a gift from God. You have been endowed by your Creator with inestimable value. Dignity and priceless value is in you. You're unique in the universe because you're created with a matchless combination of gifts, talents, strengths, personality, and physical attributes. You are unlike any other of the billions of people who preceded you or will be born after you. Never forfeit your value by becoming a victim.

CHAPTER ONE

Take a Power Pill

Think of your value and identity as a Power Pill that can't be taken away.

Yes, every person has a unique identity, a Power Pill that cannot enable another person to live within you. There's only one way it can leave your possession—if you choose to give it away. It's like a phone battery that is incompatible with a different brand of phone. It is the same way with your personal Power Pill. If you attempt to give it away by trying to meet the expectations of other people, it's useless to them while it robs you of energy and power.

Why is giving your power away a useless exercise? Because contentment and self-value are the result of an inside job. The loss of that power leaves you empty and void of inner strength.

The late Dr. Milan Johnson used to say that, when you find yourself needlessly obsessing over what others think of your actions, it means you're giving away your power. Do you want your comfort or discomfort based on the opinion of others? According to Dr. Johnson, the only people in the world who deserve that kind of excessive attention are those "in your box." These include people who would stop everything they were doing, spare no expense, and travel a great distance to attend your funeral. If you can count on more than five fingers the number of people in your life who meet that criteria, consider yourself fortunate.

How often do you give away your power? Has it become a pattern in your life? Consider these five common behaviors that are trademark signs of victim thinking.

FIVE SIGNS OF BECOMING A VOLUNTEER VICTIM

1. When we blame someone or something for where we are in life
2. When anger turns to resentment or bitterness
3. When we give in to self-pity
4. When our situation feels hopeless
5. When resignation wins

---

1. When we blame someone or something for where we are in life

The object of our blaming is the recipient of our power. This means the person, event, or negative external circumstance we hold responsible for our dissatisfaction, unproductive attitude, or destructive behavior becomes the recipient of our power. Blaming someone or something for *where we are* gives us instant access to an excuse.

2. When anger turns to resentment or bitterness

Perhaps you have experienced one of these uncomfortable moments in your workplace. You're walking down a hallway and suddenly your eyes connect with a person approaching from a distance. After a quick glance, you determine it's someone you have negative feelings toward. Every step that person draws nearer, your heart rate increases. Without conscious instruction, your entire body tightens and your teeth clench. Just before you encounter that person, you experience an unexpected surge of anxiety.

Time slows down and a conversation takes place inside your mind. *It's Susan. Of all the people who could be in the hallway today in this moment, it just had to be her. Why me? Why her? Can I turn away? Is there an*

16

exit before we meet? I'll just look down at my phone and pretend not to see her. That's ridiculous. I'll confront her. I'll ignore her. Should I say something flippant? Just keep walking and get this over with!

After Susan passes by, you find yourself reliving the reasons you feel such spite, hatred, or disgust toward her. In your mind, you replay the scenes of how badly she wronged you as you inwardly hope she gets what she deserves. It takes a few minutes to quiet your mind and return your thoughts to what you were doing before the encounter. Your past situation with Susan began with anger and grew into resentment. As a result, the wrong word, a random encounter, or the mention of her name triggers an overwhelming siege of bitterness. At that instant she owns you. And the situation owns you, too.

What happened? Merely seeing Susan dramatically turned your day on a dime. When someone has that kind of effect on you, you have already transferred your power and handed that person the capacity to determine the quality of your day.

3. **When we give in to self-pity**

When we're Living on the Shore of Status Quo, there's always a party on the beach—but it's not a luau and no one is dancing. As we draw near, we hear only sad music. That's because, on the Shore, the best-attended parties are pity parties. That's where we unveil a list of how we've been disadvantaged, disrespected, or dismissed.

When we're comfortable with victim thinking, self-pity becomes second nature. Like a myopic disease, self-pity exaggerates obstacles and turns our view inward. Rather than taking responsibility for doing what's necessary to influence the outcome in a positive manner, we protest what has happened to us. Every conversation at a "pity party" revolves around the injustice we have suffered.

Self-pity is considered victim behavior because it's an attention-seeking device designed to impress others. It's as if we're shouting, "I want you to know how special I am. I have more on my plate than you do. Being me requires an extraordinary measure of strength and character that you do not possess. I can handle it, though. Be impressed with me and the weight I must bear." When we're focused inwardly like this, we cease to care about others, even those who have suffered more than us. Then we resist empathy or compassion and simply revel in our pity parties.

4.   **When a situation feels hopeless**

We experience deep challenges in life that surfaced serious questions about the future. Hardship can lead to a long, tenuous gaze in the mirror and questions such as these: *What is the purpose of life? How long will my life be this difficult?*

Some things in life aren't fixable or resolvable, thus creating horrible dilemmas that have no concise answers or easy solutions. Still, hope can fuel perseverance and drive positive movement through the valleys of life. For most challenges, hope enables us to seek other possibilities. However, when we become a victim of our circumstances, hope fades away. Believing no other side exists ends up with refusing to consider alternatives. In this way, the absence of hope is debilitating.

5.   **When resignation wins**

We deal with two types of resignation. Formal resignation is a document that signals the end of employment. Frequently, it includes an official date when the relationship between employee and employer will cease. The second type of resignation is an inside job. Perhaps you've witnessed colleagues or co-workers still "on the job" but have clearly resigned inside. They've disengaged from passionate pursuit of excellence and are simply coasting. At some point, they've concluded they cannot influence the desired outcome. So first they give up on themselves, and then they quit their teammates, relationships, or organizations.

People caught in the web of resignation rarely bring an attitude that attracts or inspires others. In fact, their actions and overall demeanor often dampens the enthusiasm of those around them and hinders positive momentum.

Resignation goes further than hopelessness. Usually, it's hopelessness that has been acted on but in a passive-aggressive manner. People who feel hopeless give up their power to circumstances while concluding that undesirable outcomes can't be reversed. They rationalize by saying, "Why waste energy addressing them?"

Ironically, when we're in a resigned state, we've checked out on our responsibility but continue to receive compensation and benefits. This is aptly described as crawling into a self-made hole and expecting full compensation for doing so. By thinking like a victim, resignation shows irresponsibility—to us, to others, and to our organizations.

Transferring Responsibility for Self to Others

Each of these five behaviors represents an effort to transfer responsibility to someone or something else as rationale for living with an undesired reality. Rather than empowering ourselves with the freedom to shift that reality, we wait on something beyond our control as the solution to our pain, misfortune, and less-than-ideal outcomes.

THE REALITY OF CHANGE

Real change—deep authentic change—requires a great deal of energy and effort. When we become a victim, we willingly forfeit the power and energy necessary to embark on the journey of change. But when we choose to change, we won't exhibit these behaviors. And we'll experience the confidence that comes with that shift. Here's an example.

Carol suffered from Lou Gehrig's disease or ALS. When she learned her diagnosis, she knew there was no cure, no solution. For the last two years of her life, this precious lady struggled every day as this disease assaulted her body. Yet, Carol never forfeited her resolve to die with dignity, and she's representative of many of the courageous people living with ALS.

For those who knew her, Carol's journey has become a monument of inspiration. When you consider your fears, think about Carol or someone you know who has faced fear, known fear, and resolved to live courageously in spite of fear.

Carol can also teach us practical lessons. First, she was determined to squeeze something meaningful out of each day in a body that held her active mind in captivity. Her inner strength in spite of a devastating disease serves as an inspiring antithesis to a victim attitude. Her circumstances were dire. Her resolve was vibrant. Second, she did not allow her determination to be victimized by her disease. She was resilient. Finally, Carol was able to recognize the power of hope. Perhaps her greatest legacy message is this: *When you want to resign, dig deeper and choose to find hope.*

Attitude Matters

In his compelling book *Man's Search for Meaning*, the late psychologist Viktor Frankl provided a gripping account of his experiences as a prisoner in a German extermination camp during World War II. While many fellow prisoners have retold their own horrid experiences, Frankl's book reaches beyond the retelling of unbelievable suffering. Instead, it provides us with an understanding that *we can continue to grow in spite of all indignities.*[1]

Frankl, as a young psychologist, declined accepting a visa that would have allowed him to move to America where he could freely focus on his burgeoning career. Knowing his choice guaranteed future suffering within a bestial extermination camp, he opted to stay in Austria to do whatever he could to protect his father and mother. Ultimately, he lost his possessions, his parents, his wife, and his brother to death.

Writing in the preface of Frankl's book, Dr. Gordon Allport, Harvard professor of psychology, asked, "How could he, with every possession lost, every value destroyed, suffering from hunger, cold and brutality, hourly expecting extermination? How could he find life worth preserving?"[2]

In such an unimaginable environment, Frankl concluded that when life is stripped bare leaving only stark nakedness, there's one freedom that can never be taken away: *The ability to choose one's attitude.* While he saw the atrocities man is capable of visiting on others, he also witnessed mankind's capacity to walk into such evil upright, with a dignity that goes deeper than the depth of the suffering itself.

In that grim hell, Frankl realized his purpose was to help people reclaim their own purpose and dignity. As he wrote, "Everything can be taken from a man but one thing: the last of the human freedoms—to choose one's attitude in any given set of circumstances, to choose one's own way."

---

[1] From *Man's Search for Meaning* by Viktor E. Frankl. Copyright © 1959, 1962, 1984, 1992 by Viktor E. Frankl. Reprinted by permission of Beacon Press, Boston.
[2] Ibid.

THE REALITY OF CHANGE

Lift Your Head and Look Ahead

Typically, people in The Land of Status Quo have allowed themselves to be consumed by their current predicament, often forming a distorted view of its overwhelming immensity. No doubt you have observed people paralyzed by a sense of hopelessness. They spend their thoughts and energies, mentally protesting the unfairness of their situation. Many question repeatedly, "Why did it happen to me?"

Yet, when individuals identify timeless principles that served them well through earlier crises and then refocused on adhering to them, a new sense of perspective begins to grow. It's not possible to plunge into The Land of Status Quo while simultaneously being committed to a higher purpose that extends beyond the moment.

Breaking out of the paralysis of status quo nearly always begins when we stop obsessing on our own difficulties. Rather, we seek ways to serve others in the midst of our difficulties. In doing so, we realize that a purpose exists greater than ourselves, and we identify with that purpose. We focus on the collective memories of when our lives were attuned to it. That way, we can develop a depth of meaning and responsibility that gives us the strength to move forward in spite of palpable challenges.

Prepare to Leave the Shore

What does changing the outcome of your life require? Facing up to the fact that the biggest obstacles to change have little to do with circumstances and much to do with doubts and fears. If you are serious about making a decision to leave the shore, recognize those obstacles, face your fears, and refuse to think like a victim.

Prepare to leave The Land of Status Quo.

REFLECT AND RESPOND

1. How would you describe Living on the Shore of Status Quo?
2. Describe a situation when you behaved like a "volunteer victim."
3. Describe the most positive aspects of your attitude toward change.
4. Describe the most negative aspects of your attitude toward change.

Remember This

**As you begin to contemplate positive change in your life,
you will experience an uncomfortable tension.**

THE REALITY OF CHANGE

CHAPTER TWO

LEAVING THE LAND
OF STATUS QUO

"Everyone thinks of changing the world,
but no one thinks of changing himself."

-Leo Tolstoy

THE REALITY OF CHANGE

Todd's Story

Todd was a bright, energetic young man with an inner drive to do something meaningful with his life. Since high school graduation, he worked toward a college degree in construction management. He enjoyed custom home construction work, but the industry was going through difficult recessionary times. He had been laid off from two companies as he struggled to find work. With a wife and a child at home, he was continually worrying about job security. Todd didn't like the feeling that his future was up in the air. He hadn't imagined living through this constant threat of joblessness. Indeed, he dreamed of more for himself and his family.

Then Todd caught a break. When he was twenty-five, it seemed as though he was about to turn the corner and establish himself in the industry as a construction manager. A custom homebuilder with a stellar reputation offered him a job as a supervisor. Even better, the opportunity came with full support for Todd to continue his education.

But the euphoria was short-lived. After only one year, the volatile housing market claimed another victim. Todd's company slipped into crisis and despite his excellent work record, his position was eliminated. Soon after Todd's departure, the company closed its doors. The road toward construction management became a dead end, and he took a job as a server at a franchise restaurant. To say that Todd was despondent would be an understatement. Frustrated and tired, he felt sorry for himself and his family.

Sometimes, in the darkest times, a fresh spark of hope emerges. It may only be tiny, but it can become a powerful precursor for change. Todd's spark of hope came in the form of an aspiration that had been buried for a long time. He'd always dreamed of becoming a helicopter pilot but had repressed this desire, frequently dismissing it as a fantasy. The voices of self-doubt reminded him he'd never be able to master such a challenging profession. The few times he risked telling others about his desire, friends and family quickly reminded him of his inadequacies. They tossed out questions like verbal hand grenades. How would he afford the sizable training expenses? How would he support his family and go to school at the same time? What if he failed?

Questions and self-doubt led to concluding that flying helicopters was not an option. Working in an unstable profession would have to be his "lot in life." Todd reluctantly let go of this hope.

Every spark needs a little help to become a flame. Similarly, every successful life change needs an initial push—one that provides necessary momentum. For Todd, the spark came when he was laid off at the restaurant. At first, it seemed like another devastating blow to Todd and his family. How could it get any worse? That's when he resolved he wouldn't settle for this type of uncertainty any longer. With support from his wife, he mapped out his plans to pursue his career as a helicopter pilot. He declared to family and friends that, no matter how difficult the task or the financial sacrifices, "I am doing this!" The pain of repeated layoffs gave Todd the courage to act in spite of his fear, and he made the commitment to leave The Land of Status Quo.

You will revisit Todd's journey later in this book. For now, consider his story an example of someone who bravely left the shore to pursue a new life.

What is needed to move forward? In a word: motivation—a mixture of inspiration, determination, and provocation.

What's Required to Leave the Land of Status Quo?

We will never change without the will to change. We might think identifying the benefits of positive change should be sufficient. In fact, most young leaders believe that an idea will succeed simply on the merits of the idea. We may still carry the notion that the better the idea, the easier it will be to persuade others to accept a proposed change. We assume that people will naturally understand the value of change and get onboard.

But before exploring the three effective motives for change, it's important to understand one of the most formidable barriers to change: safety.

Is it Safe to Change?

In his groundbreaking work "The Hierarchy of Needs" (Figure 1), Abraham Maslow, the father of American psychology, helped us understand that human beings tend to focus their intense energies on areas of critical needs not being met in their lives. All humans yearn for the same things.

Maslow defined and prioritized the various levels of need that all people possess regardless of age, gender, culture, geography, race, or religion. (There are no exceptions, assuming the presence of relatively non-pathological people in the population.)

FIGURE 1

The bottom of the pyramid refers to physiological survival needs. This implies that, at this stage, we don't think about anything else if our basic needs for air, food, and water aren't supplied. For example, if we haven't eaten food in two weeks, it's unlikely to assume we'd be thinking about how to strengthen our positive impact on humanity.

Once our physiological needs are met consistently—the stomach is full, the lungs have clean air, and we have plenty of water—we tend to take those things for granted. That's when we turn our attention toward more important things on higher levels of the pyramid.

Maslow suggested the next important area of need is safety, which extends beyond the physical realm. This means we want to be warm, dry, clothed, and out of harm's way. However, it also means we crave predictability. We find security in a steady rhythm that allows us to live and plan our lives with a good degree of certainty. People have a need for control (or the illusion of it) to feel safe.

Here, the relationship between change and human nature gets dicey. It's natural to avoid anything that feels threatening. Avoiding the threat of physical harm is an obvious response, yet threat avoidance can be complex. Essentially, change involves a commitment to a perceived loss of control, and that feels threatening. Change means surrendering oneself to uncertainty, and that seems hazardous to the brain. It wants a guaranteed reward, yet change typically provides more risks than guarantees.

The process invites us to exchange solid ground for the sea of change. Change ushers in risk and uncertainty, trading from the known to the unknown. Not only does such a movement set off a warning signal in the brain, it also triggers an immediate fear of loss. This is an example of the internal messaging that drives the anxiety and fear associated with change.

THE REALITY OF CHANGE

At its core, change can cause us to conclude we're moving from a safe place to an immediate threat. While we might understand why we won't cross the first line of Maslow's hierarchy until our physical needs are met, why might we struggle to understand how the same principle applies to the second line? It's a part of being human.

Know this: At the core of our existence—built within our emotional DNA—*resisting change is a natural, inevitable response to perceived threats.* Accept that change represents a strange paradox—that is, it feels like a threat while at that same time, it's life-giving. Without change, stagnation and decline are inevitable.

While the need to resist change is an engrained response to a perceived threat, Maslow's work has revealed a valuable perspective on The Reality of Change. A perceived need for absolute safety can become a *barrier* to other needs. Therefore, fear of change can become a substantial obstacle. Remember, the lower levels of Maslow's hierarchy provide for physiological needs and safety while the higher levels offer the rewards of social relationships, self-esteem, and self-actualization. Safety can stand between your present existence and fulfillment in other areas of life. That means to reach the height of your potential requires stretching beyond your comfort zone.

For Maslow, the highest need—self-actualization—happens when individuals fully use their abilities in a way that creates a significant, profoundly positive impact on others. It also creates a deep sense of personal meaning in one's life. Self-actualization means the ability to look in the mirror and know that *you matter.* The reward? It feels gratifying to know you're making a difference, that your life is better and you influence others for good.

CHAPTER TWO

Unceasing Commitment to Growth

Ironically, Maslow discovered that only a small percentage of people fulfill this universal need for self-actualization. Why? Because it's a difficult transition. As Maslow understood it, self-actualization requires a serious commitment to personal development; it's impossible to realize self-actualization without it. People need self-awareness, self-discovery, and a desire for transformation. Yet this evolution cannot occur without an openness and commitment to change. And while not all change leads to growth, no growth can occur without it.

At this level, people are in a place of constant tension regarding change. So before completely unplugging your internal warning system, understand that having a desire for safety is not *bad*. Self-awareness allows you to recognize when legitimate concerns for safety slowly morph into a significant barrier to personal development. An unhealthy obsession with risk-free living will stifle any exhilaration, passion, and opportunity for impact. You cannot experience this without embracing change as a constant.

To experience "greatness" requires a willingness to release fear, become comfortable with being uncomfortable, and embrace change as a requirement for making a difference. *If you cannot move beyond your basic need to avoid tension, discomfort, or anxiety as a condition of feeling safe, you will aim for an acceptable level of predictability at the expense of maximizing your potential.*

So what motivates people to cross the line and create change in their lives? If a desire for safety is so strong, then how will they overcome it? Many of these factors contribute to a robust motivation for Leaving the Land of Status Quo—that is, escape from the present, move into the future, follow the lure of more money and opportunities to grow and develop, and yearn to make a difference in the world. Each of these ideas has something to contribute to your motivation.

It's not possible to cover an exhaustive list, but the following three motives for change deserve closer examination.

THREE MOTIVES FOR CHANGE

1. We change to ease the pain.
2. We change to capture potential.
3. We change to continue productivity.

---

1. MOTIVATION ONE: We Change to Ease the Pain

Perspective matters. It is not uncommon to hear older folks talk about returning to the "good old days." Back then, they muse, life was simpler, slower, and sweeter. Change has stolen these things. Yet, if returning to the "good old days" means using outdoor toilets, having no electricity, enduring summers without air conditioning, or getting to a destination on horseback, then maybe change isn't so bad.

Do you romanticize about the past? You can fall into the same trap when it comes to the present. After all, it's far too easy to convince yourself that life is fine. Because life without pain doesn't exist, developing a proper perspective is essential.

Change is a process that's both a necessity for the human spirit to soar as well as a reality that rubs against the grain of our basic human needs. We cannot live *without* it but are often afraid to live *with* it. It always begins with an answer to the personal question, "Why should I change?" Your answer becomes your motivation to change.

Knowing that change goes against the grain of basic human nature, the first motive for change is often to find relief from significant pain.

The majority of people seek major change only when the pain of staying the same becomes greater than the pain of changing. The pain or discomfort of a current situation can force us into a corner that's no longer tolerable and we become desperate for a way out. In that moment, we gain clarity and see that The Land of Status Quo is no longer the best alternative.

Organizations Act as People Do

What's true for individuals is true for organizations. After all, organizations are collections of people. Some organizations crave safety and avoid threats more than others. These organizations build up a deep resistance to change as if it were a part of their DNA. Conversely, some companies welcome constant change. Instead of viewing it as a necessary evil, they see it as an opportunity to thrive. When organizations postpone change until the pain of the present is unbearable, they forfeit the opportunity to become industry leaders. Such organizations might manage to survive, but they will seldom be leaders in their categories.

At the organizational level, when change becomes a tool of last resort, it's often too little too late. Why does this phenomenon exist? Too often these companies are free falling before their leaders fully acknowledge the decline. Reversing the sheer force of the downward inertia is challenging at best.

In addition, leaders stuck in change-resistant thinking rarely generate entirely fresh, radical, systemic strategies necessary for survival. Change efforts in organizations that are driven by a desire to cease pain typically seek a deep result with minimal change. Frequently, their leaders require new energy and ideas from an outsider who isn't trapped in the culture of self-limiting thinking that failed the organization.

Organizational Change to Ease the Pain

Two well-known companies that committed to change to stop pain are the Eastman Kodak Company and General Motors. Let's examine their situations.

Eastman Kodak

Eastman Kodak, one of the most innovative companies of the 20th century, experienced a deep decline since the late 1990s when it needed to shift from film into digital photography services. The company, notorious for its change-resistant culture, attempted moderate changes, which proved ineffective as the digital transformation rendered many of its star products obsolete. Having filed for bankruptcy in 2012 and laid off thousands of employees, experts predicted that even if the bleeding had been stopped, the company would only represent a shadow of its former self. The journey of Kodak during that era provides a classic case study of "too little too late" as a survival tool to escape intolerable pain.

General Motors

General Motors is the rare exception of a company surviving a free fall but only after it changed to stop the pain. Yes, it did have extraordinary help. As a condition of receiving a federal government bailout of 25 billion dollars in exchange for 61 percent of its stock, the company was forced to accept these conditions:

- Conduct a complete reorganization,
- Agree to file for bankruptcy,

- Accept an entirely new leadership team of no "car guys,"
- Replace the previous board of directors, and
- Radically downsize the company's operations.

It's a reasonable assumption that such deep change would not have occurred without this highly controversial intervention from the U.S. government.

Deep corporate change usually faces more barriers than individual change. That's because individuals committed to personal change compete only against themselves and require just their personal commitment. On the other hand, organizational change requires the support of many while competing against other businesses, especially those willing to make timely, appropriate changes to maintain their edge. Even with appropriate change, the future success of the company may be out of reach due to competitive marketplace realities and missed opportunities.

Case Study: Personal Change to Ease the Pain

A few years ago, Joe was a second-generation leader whose family owned multiple retail franchises. While a gifted businessman, Joe possessed an extremely strong ego—a trait that was instrumental in his pattern of not receiving constructive criticism well.

Joe was known for his despotic leadership style. Each of the stores he led shared unacceptably high turnover—far beyond even the normal revolving-door employment patterns within his industry. Profits had been affected to the degree the corporate leaders of the national franchising company asked consultants to intervene.

During the course of their work together, it became clear Joe was obsessed with proving to others, and to himself, that he was an effective leader who followed in his late father's footsteps. He ignored suggestions and counsel from anyone who tried to help him with his tyrannical leadership style. Ironically, as he confided, he felt terrified of failure.

In Joe's mind, reaching out for help to change his leadership approach would be an admission of failure. Thus, his fragile ego kept him mired in an unhealthy leadership pattern. Finally, when three of his stores were placed on notice by the parent organization, his fear of failure overcame his need to project an air of success. In deep pain, he admitted he needed help and was willing to face his limitations to help turn the health of his business around.

For Joe, the pain of changing himself finally overshadowed the pain of staying the same.

2. **MOTIVATION TWO: We Change to Capture Potential**

The rationale for change, as described previously, is stimulated greatly by outside pressure. When that becomes greater than the pressure from the inside, we become more willing to consider change.

The second motive for change begins on the inside. *The desire to capture more personal leadership potential is a powerful motivator for positive change.* It begins with one's core values and principles as well as making personal transformation a priority. Personal transformation requires viewing life through a different lens.

Evidence of this motivation is rare, because far too many people are "fear based" rather than "principle led" in their decision-making. Change for the sake of capturing potential is not an act of desperation but an exercise of stewardship. In fact, this type of change is driven by those who want to be full stewards of their opportunities, talents, and abilities. When we see future potential, then we feel energized, not paralyzed, and a pursuit of excellence emerges from within.

A coach described this kind of change as the distinction between "champions" and "commoners." Inside the heart of the "champion" (either a person or an organization) is a burning fire to *be* more and *claim* more. Think of it as the antithesis of the old idiom, "If it ain't broke, don't fix it." Once we elevate our gaze to a vision that captures our hearts, "average" becomes unacceptable. From there, emotional buy-in is kindled and a new mindset is born.

Despite motivation's compelling nature, don't think fear is totally vanquished. Yes, champions acknowledge the existence of fear but their principles override it. They reinterpret their failures and never consider them final because they're propelled by internal conviction rather than outer affirmation. Simply stated, champions regard failures as useful information for the journey toward change.

The Green Bay Packers football team would fall into the category of an organization seeking change to capture potential. Located in Green Bay, Wisconsin, a small city of 104,000 people, the Packers have been the envy of other National Football League's (NFL) organizations for years. With the support of a rabid national fan base, the Packers have consistently occupied the upper tier of elite teams, both in on-field performance and financial stability. Part of the team's success lies behind an unceasing commitment to change for the sake of being better—that is, change to capture potential.

A few years ago, the sports world watched with keen interest when the Packers chose to trade three-time league MVP (Most Valuable Player), longtime icon, and fan favorite quarterback Brett Favre. Lionized for his role in the turnaround of the NFL franchise's fortunes and in leading the team back to consecutive Super Bowl championships, the expected backlash came down severely. Many casual observers were shocked that the team would jettison arguably the greatest player in its celebrated history following one of his most productive seasons.

Yet the Packers' leaders saw that greater success would occur if they addressed the delicate issue of an aging quarterback who would soon lose the competition with Father Time. Further, they believed it had a potential superstar in its young, unproven backup quarterback, Aaron Rodgers, who'd spent three years waiting for his chance.

Favre was known as The Gunslinger because he wasn't afraid to improvise. He'd commonly deviate from the carefully scripted game plan with a reckless abandon. Some hailed this as a virtue and others criticized it as a vice. Yet his erratic, impulsive decision-making had hurt the team's results on many occasions. In the end, many regarded Favre as a prima donna who resisted buy-in of the philosophy and leadership of the new general manager and head coach.

The Packers searched within its organization, considered the present, and raised their sights toward the future. The conclusion? The team couldn't maintain its current success if difficult choices weren't made. Certainly, Packers' leaders understood the implausibility of reclaiming a Super Bowl title without making changes. Given their relentless commitment to excellence, they made the gutsy, controversial move to break ties with Favre. Despite howls of protest, time proved this decision correct. Brilliant young Aaron Rodgers soon gained the full appreciation of the Packers' nation. He led them to another Super Bowl title while helping the team earn all-time record profits. While this occurred, Favre was faltering in his final season with another team.

What was the Packers' motivation to change, even when it felt uncomfortable? *Capturing potential.* This requires leaders to deal with sensitive issues and people—the organizational sacred cows. These can be long-held traditions, methods, or people that at one time served the organization in a powerful manner. With the march of time, those traditions or methods may no longer work.

Organizations wanting to experience successful change have to face sacred-cow issues. They must address them strategically, with sensitivity, and with the full support of the organization's top leaders. Remember, the motivation to deal with sensitive issues is not personal; rather, it aligns with core values and reaches toward a brighter vision.

Ultimately, whoever wins the battle of the sacred cows will have the true leadership influence in the organization, regardless of title or position. Conversely, the failure to effectively address sacred-cow issues will afford an organization a permanent address in The Land of Status Quo. Change opens the door to greater potential. It's always driven by courage from deep within.

3   MOTIVATION THREE: We Change to Continue Productivity

Newton's Law says bodies at rest cannot remain at rest. Directly related to that, human life progresses or declines with no in-between stage. Ultimately, you live in a world that expects results. You feel the pressure to either grow or go. You will either be conformed from the *outside in* or transformed from the *inside out.*

The third motivation for change draws from wisdom about the dynamics of life. If you are wise, you'll be motivated to *change for continued productivity.* To resist a decrease in yield, therefore, requires changing.

THE REALITY OF CHANGE

By now, you understand that change can be resisted but not stopped. You can't decide whether or not you will change; rather, your choice narrows down to this question: *Will I make change my ally or will I declare it my enemy?*

Refuse to Change and You Forfeit Productivity

Chuck was a skilled draftsman who parlayed his talents into a 25-year career. The unfortunate news is that he could have made it into a 45-year career *if he had been willing to stay relevant in his field.*

A few years ago, Chuck bragged he would never be forced to use the computerized methods of drawing that were emerging. He refused to learn software that enabled him to complete his drawings using the latest technology. Slowly, Chuck fell behind and eventually couldn't keep up with his cohorts. They could churn out precise drawings with greater detail in a more timely and efficient manner than Chuck could. His productivity dropped until he lost his job.

Chuck felt bitter that his firm had treated him so poorly. In his mind, he had been loyal, and that loyalty was not returned. In reality, his refusal to change did not exhibit loyalty to his organization. Rather, it turned him into a liability that affected the quality and the efficiency of his employer.

In this way, Chuck was determined to stay entrenched in The Land of Status Quo. The place that offered a false sense of stability ultimately became his professional grave. Because he refused to change, he lost the flexibility of having productive options for his future. Chuck had attempted to control the march of change. Unfortunately, he lost control over his future and enabled others to determine it for him.

CHAPTER TWO

Embracing Change to Increase Productivity

Here's how Karen learned to embrace change. She owned multiple McDonald's restaurants in the Detroit area. Her most profitable operation was located in an upscale suburb heavily populated with high-income professionals. Despite her success, she decided to sell this property and move the operation to an adjacent village.

When asked about her reasoning, she said in the previous month, the city voted to restrict restaurants from operating a drive-thru. At the time, drive-thru business accounted for 55 percent of her store's revenue. This ruling would effectively eliminate Karen's ability to grow the business. As she considered the trajectory of future fixed costs, she gained insight into her best plan for continued growth.

Karen chose to operate from a position of strong momentum, not a position of decline. In the short term, it was a difficult and costly decision. However, she wasn't concerned about the short term. Instead, she focused on continued productivity. And she wasn't willing to wait until her store's productivity declined to make a decision.

As a result of her foresight, in the first year, her new store set record profits within her operation. How? A main factor was the significantly increased revenue from her new drive-thru location.

REFLECT AND RESPOND

1. Think of a time when you made a positive change in your life. Describe your motivation(s) for making the change.
2. Identify a specific change you are contemplating today.
3. Describe your motivation for change.
    a. Do you desire to ease the pain of the status quo?
    b. Do you desire to capture potential?
    c. Do you desire to continue productivity?

Remember This

Change, at its very core, can cause people to conclude they're moving from a safe place to an immediate threat. If you cannot progress beyond your basic need to avoid tension, discomfort, or anxiety as a condition of feeling safe, what happens? You will aim for an acceptable level of predictability at the expense of maximizing your potential.

CHAPTER THREE

THE PRICE OF CROSSING THE SHORELINE
PURCHASING YOUR TICKET

"Taking a new step, uttering a new word,
is what people fear most."

-Fyodor Dostoyevsky

THE REALITY OF CHANGE

Are You Serious about Change?

Change is costly. Leaving The Land of Status Quo is a big deal. Don't underestimate the significance of departing from it.

Hopefully, you have broadened your understanding of the three major motivations for change. The first rationale—changing to cease pain—is motivated by misery, *powerful gut-wrenching misery*. The second rationale—changing to capture potential—is motivated by *inward conviction fueled by deeply held values and principles*. The third rationale—changing to continue productivity—is motivated by *wisdom, insight, and seasoned discernment*.

Once you're ready to move, it's time to consider your first steps.

Purchase the Ticket and Get on the Boat

You talked about change.

> *You confessed the need for change.*

> *You feel sure you're ready for change.*

> *You haven't made the change.*

> *You are not alone.*

Anger lurks beneath the surface and exists on a continuum. Some anger is due to failure. While failed attempts at change are easy to access in your memory, deeper wounds are harder to identify. Those wounds come from failed intentions and are linked to attempts to change that never got off the ground. You thought about change, but didn't truly launch a change *initiative*. Now you need a plan of action.

Change is a popular subject: books are written about it and the media grabs your attention. As a result, you feel guilty. You have paused more than once to glance at an ad and wonder whether a short-cut solution to better health, weight loss, or personal wealth might be worth a few dollars. Every day, millions of people sit around in a café, sip coffee, and talk about what needs to change. But what's the story at the end of the day? *There is a difference between a dream and a plan. Shortcuts are not the answer.*

A serious commitment to change includes four recognizable steps.

FOUR UNMISTAKABLE STEPS SIGNAL A TRUE LAUNCH FROM THE SHORE:

1. Making a personal commitment.
2. Declaring the commitment to another.
3. Creating a specific, realistic, and actionable plan.
4. Initiating execution of the plan.

1. Making a personal commitment.

Commitment. This is the most important step in any successful change process. Opportunities abound. But opportunities possess an ethereal quality that's only substantiated when we move toward them in earnest. They remain on the periphery of life until we make a commitment. In business, we've learned the importance of a pledge made in good faith. It's more than talk; it's attached to character and anchored by integrity.

For many years, a pledge in business was sealed with a handshake. Without debating the origin and evolution of the handshake, consider that personal nature of commitment. When we make a commitment, it's more than words, for it's the heart *behind* the words that will move us forward. Real change that connects head and heart begins with an internal commitment to change. More than actions, a commitment represents an attitude, a new perspective, and a view of the world from a different mindset. We let our commitments open our senses to a new realm of possibilities.

As an example, a colleague of mine made a commitment to change his life, to leave his safe but unsatisfying career and enroll in an executive leadership program at Notre Dame University. The commitment began as a dream for a better life. In turn, the dream spurred an interior conversation. He confided that he was scared to death, but he mustered the courage to make the commitment anyway.

Midway through the program, no employment opportunities had surfaced, yet he was determined to persevere. By the time he graduated, though, he had so many opportunities open up to him that it took a few months to sort them out. When he stopped by to see me, a smile broadened his face and he confided, "I feel like I'm in the catbird's seat. I had no idea that the position I took would have ever been possible."

The value of your first step to commit increases over time. As my colleague learned, initiative is the precursor to a fulfilled dream.

2. Declaring the commitment to another.

The possibilities for success improve significantly when we have the courage to share the news of our commitment with another person and invite positive peer pressure. With each step in the change process, we boost our personal accountability and thereby increase our potential for success. We are not serious about a commitment until there's a willingness to create a personal network for accountability. This means being willing to be accountable to ourselves and others. It requires being explicit while enabling someone else to ask the hard questions.

Beyond the increased accountability, there's another benefit of declaring a commitment to someone else: *Change moves from the inside to the outside.* Remember, failed intentions can poison a person's belief system. But when we share our goals with another person, we have taken the next step toward change. Know this: The deepest changes are typically those that come with significant obstacles and challenges, and they're rarely achieved without engaging a supportive community.

Here's an example. During a leadership development process, an executive was given the task of informing three trusted individuals of her plan to achieve a long-held personal goal. She had taken the first step; she'd committed to fulfill her dream of publishing a book. After twenty years as an executive, she had assembled a collection of colorful stories and life lessons that were tucked away in journals and notebooks in a file cabinet. So her next step was to pull the stories together and arrange them in a logical sequence. For years, she had failed to move beyond her good intentions, so enlisting the help of three others to keep her accountable was her next step. It was time to declare her commitment to others.

However, when the due date came to confirm her declaration, she failed to show up for the session. A quick inquiry revealed that her absence was an attempt to avoid facing the truth. She had not fulfilled her task and had never connected with any of her three designated people. She didn't even declare her commitment to them. When asked for a reason, she gave this classic answer: "I wasn't about to tell them about my commitment. I'm not ready. Once I told them, I would be accountable. I feared that I could not or would not be successful, so I kept it to myself."

By not declaring her commitment to others, she had not truly committed to *herself.* Unfortunately, as time marches on, her journals and notebooks remain in the cabinet and the potential impact of her insights is locked away.

3. **Creating a specific, realistic and actionable plan.**

    A dream without a plan is merely an idea that's imprisoned in your mind. The odds for success increase exponentially when you develop a clear, thoughtful, deliberate plan of action. Every journey includes a time of departure and arrival.

    More than that, being serious about change includes setting specific markers in time. When will you begin? When will you evaluate your progress? When will you arrive?

    Every journey portends both expected and unexpected challenges. A strong plan will carefully anticipate physical and emotional barriers that stand in the way of completing the dream. When challenges are anticipated, they become less threatening. Someone who frequently flies in airplanes doesn't get disturbed by a little turbulence because it's expected. When resistance comes as a surprise, it seems more threatening.

    How can you lessen the intimidation that often accompanies obstacles? By preparing in advance. Specifically, make a realistic list of potential roadblocks that threaten your success, then construct a few tactical action plans to overcome problems before they become a crisis.

Not only does this provide for success when the obstacles materialize, it reduces fear of the unknown.

Much resistance to change is fueled by emotional tension. Creating a plan to overcome that tension opens the door for executing meaningful change.

4. **Initiating execution of the plan.**

A commitment without execution is only a false promise. It's far too easy to stall at this particular phase because of some mitigating fear. Many plans lie dormant year after year. Remember the ominous list of fears that dominate Living on the Shore of Status Quo? Just because you've taken a few positive steps toward change, these fears won't magically disappear:

- A fear of discomfort
- A fear of failure
- A fear of disappointment
- A fear of the unknown
- A fear that you are not enough

In fact, you can add another "strange" fear to the list:

- A fear that you will succeed

Because successful change deepens questions about the unknown, it's wise to ask, "How will success affect my identity? My relationships? My future?" The obvious cure for fear is courage, which is a necessary precursor to action. But nothing substitutes for action. Courage alone isn't the answer for overcoming fear. And by waiting for sufficient courage to dispel all fear, we remain with the masses Living on the Shore of Status Quo. Instead, recognize that *action* is the antidote to fear. Taking one step at a time increases courage with every movement forward. Nothing weakens the grip of fear like momentum.

Why These Four Steps are Important

As you rehearse the value of each step in your mind, recognize how the four unmistakable steps signal a true launch from the shore. When you make a serious commitment to change, these four steps will become woven together into a web of accountability. This web of accountability doesn't alter The Reality of Change, nor will it erase the formidable forces against change. Yet having a solid plan equips you for what lies ahead.

When you implement the four steps, you signal your launch from the shore. You've been warned that challenges await anyone who's willing to initiate change. Simply know that the challenges ahead are predictable, observable, and inevitable. These challenges are not isolated to you. As you will discover, they're not personal, although they will often appear to be so. Rather, they're part of the process that occurs once you take responsibility for gaining a new outcome in your life.

Your next challenge requires determination and focus. It's time to stay the course.

REFLECT AND RESPOND

1. Are you ready to move forward with a change initiative?
2. If so, it's time to develop a Personal Plan to Change.

Make a personal commitment to yourself:

I commit to _____

_____

_____on this date_____.

Declare the commitment to another:

I shared my commitment with _____

_____on this date_____.

Create a specific, realistic, and actionable plan:

Record each significant step and method of evaluating completion, along with a person who will provide accountability.

Initiate execution of the plan:

I began my planned change on this date_____.
With completion of this step on _____.

THE REALITY OF CHANGE

Remember This

Acknowledge the difference between a dream and a plan. A serious commitment to change includes four recognizable steps. Remember, taking shortcuts on these steps simply doesn't work.

PART TWO:

STAYING THE COURSE ON STORMY SEAS

"We must always remember with gratitude and admiration the first sailors who steered their vessels through storms and mists, and increased our knowledge of the lands of ice in the South."

-Roald Amundsen, Antarctic Explorer

THE REALITY OF CHANGE

CHAPTER FOUR

UNWANTED STOWAWAYS
BEWARE THE NAYSAYERS

They shout from the shore, but they live inside of your head.

"Your business and your life will change when you really, really get it
that some people are not going to change, no matter what you do, and
that still others have a vested interest in being destructive."

-Henry Cloud

THE REALITY OF CHANGE

Unexpected Negativity

You're on your way. You've stepped out. You've moved on. Whether you have been on a magnificent cruise or simply watched a majestic ocean liner leave the port, you can probably envision a dramatic launch amid a swell of cheers and confetti. It's not likely you expect that kind of send-off when you begin a change initiative. However, it's also not likely you're prepared for the dearth of enthusiasm. If you expect everyone to be proud and excited about the new direction in your life, you're not alone. It's natural to anticipate a measure of congratulations when you muster the courage to move in a positive direction. That's why it's so surprising when you strain to hear a few cheers from the shore. No matter how often it happens, you'll still find it surprising.

It's a big deal when your moment of truth arrives and you take responsibility for a facet of your life. Who will acknowledge your bold step toward a fresh start? The response can be shocking. Not only is the lack of praise absent, it seems like naysayers gather like storm clouds on a humid summer day. These naysayers descend on you to offer impassioned advice why you should not, could not, and will not move forward with your intentions. The lack of praise may catch you off guard but unexpected negativity is even more shocking.

After hearing the barrage of "well-intentioned" negativity, you may find yourself thinking, "I didn't want their advice. I didn't need it or ask for it. I'm making a positive change! Why are these people getting involved when it isn't their business?" Actually, attacks are not unusual. *In fact, if you plan to navigate the stormy seas of change, you must prepare for the inevitable attempts to discourage your progress and poison your plans.* Not only do these naysayers make *your* business *their* business, they actually believe *your* business *is their* business. Your decision to change something in your personal life or business can touch a nerve, causing them to refuse to be silent.

Idol Talk or Just Idle Talk

What does a talented young singer do with big dreams? It always begins with the first step. She envisioned the big stage. Family members and friends recognized her talent but struggled with the dream to explore a new musical frontier. They only saw a little girl who could sing.

What happened when she shared her dream? How eager she was to share.

Given the intensity of her focus, the spark was growing into a fire. She was ready to invest her time, energy, and passion into action.

She gathered her thoughts, mustered her courage, and shared her dream. As the details of her dream rippled out through family, friends, and acquaintances, a litany of non-supportive reactions swelled. Each response contained a common thread. Her dreams were just fantasies. She wasn't realistic about her potential. In their estimation, she was overreaching what was possible.

In spite of the clamor among the skeptics, she persevered. She rose above the noise and refused to be dissuaded by those who doubted the viability of her quest. Does this sound like a fictional story? Each aspect of the story is true. In fact, it continues after a first-place finish in the groundbreaking reality TV show *American Idol* and her ongoing career success. It began with a dream that, when shared, triggered a chorus of naysayers.

When you leave the shore, expect to hear some noise.

Take a few moments and ponder your own experiences. Perhaps your initial enthusiasm about a new adventure has met considerable pushback.

Maybe you have participated in raining on someone else's parade. When it's easy to be supportive and encouraging of someone who dares to pursue a dream or a new life direction, why does the negative drown out the positive?

Humble Pie

Everybody loved Mabel, soon to be an octogenarian. She was a vivacious, fun, attractive woman who took pride in maintaining a youthful appearance. She also took pride in baking delicious pies. Mostly, she enjoyed the attention she received for her disciplined approach to diet and health. And she didn't mind at all when people bragged about either that or her pies.

Mabel was active in a small rural church congregation in the Midwest. On any given week, she'd be participating in a number of church functions. If you observed her closely, you would notice a peculiar pattern. Whenever one of the older ladies in the congregation would mention she was dieting to lose weight, Mabel showered her with her irresistible pies. The pattern became so predictable that people in the church joked about how to entice Mabel to bake her scrumptious pies through dieting conversations.

She clearly had a habit of sabotaging the healthy eating habits of those she deemed a threat to sharing her attention. In this specific instance, a deep insecurity prompted these attempts to undermine others' efforts to improve their physical appearance.

In your life, you can be certain whenever you announce a significant change or step in your life that someone will say something non-constructive about it. The bolder the step, the stronger the reaction will be. Bank on it. In fact, some will cheer for your failure or even try to dampen the desired outcome. Some methods and motivations are deeply troubling while others are humorous and some quite absurd. To be bold in your journey requires being aware of the potentially damaging effects naysayers could have.

How can you neutralize the impact of negativity? By understanding that the greatest threat to successful change will never come from naysayers. As long as the storm remains outside the ship, the boat will continue to float. Your greatest responsibility as an agent of change is to guard your thoughts, protect your mind. That means don't personalize attacks that come your way. This isn't easy, especially when they come from those closest to you. You crave the support of family members and friends; you want them to be proud of your commitment to change. When you must endure their doubts and dissent, it's easy to take their painful comments personally. *Don't do it.*

The moment you find yourself feeling resentful about another person's lack of support or negative response, stop and consider whether you're willing to divert energy away from your efforts to change. If you transfer your focus from positive change toward your resentment, you *will* suffer some negative effects. Initially, you could experience a drain in your mental and emotional energy. In addition, your level of stress and anxiety will begin to swell. If they go unchecked, you will transfer your own power and responsibility for your success to that individual.

Personalizing Criticism—Agents of Change Don't Do It!

Leaders who are effective change agents learn not to personalize the negative reactions of others, even if those reactions were intended to be personal. Instead, they step back and reclassify their words, seeking to strip away the paralyzing power of criticism. What should you do? Regard what they say as "information," then determine how you will evaluate that information. Their efforts in response to your commitment to elicit a positive change can actually be more about *them* than it is about *you.*

THE REALITY OF CHANGE

Refusing to personalize criticism is one of the most critical leadership competencies related to The Reality of Change. Think of internalized criticism like a boat taking on water. To sustain positive change momentum requires maintaining a vigilant posture toward personal criticism and not letting it sink your boat.

Remember, criticism can be constructive or destructive. The only way to receive the good and reject the bad is to develop your ability to keep the information outside in an objective area before receiving it. Again, treat criticism as "information" to be examined before allowing it inside.

To clarify, information may be accurate or helpful even if it feels uncomfortable to hear. You, however, have complete control of whether you regard that information as data to be processed, acted on, or ignored. *The worst possible choice you can make is to allow others' words to define your value as a human being.*

Crab in the Bucket Syndrome

Did you live near a stream when you were a kid? If so, you may have experienced the joy of catching a small crayfish. These crab-like creatures are a lot of fun to capture.

Catching crayfish begins by meticulously turning over a few rocks and waiting for the water to be clear enough to spot them nestled into the creek bottom. Gradually you must slip your hand into the water behind the crayfish and grab them as they quickly back up. If you place a few of them in an old coffee can, you can observe a strange phenomenon. One or two of the crayfish will attempt to climb out of the bucket, and the other creatures will reach up to grab them and thwart their escape. It's not as though the little spoilers are trying to get out of the can; they're simply preventing the others from climbing out.

CHAPTER FOUR

This "crab in the bucket syndrome" is readily observable in humans because it's the same pattern that occurs during the change process. Whenever you declare a bold change to move out of your current reality, expect someone to make the effort to pull you back. It's also important to understand why much of the resistance may come from people who genuinely care about you. Their motives for providing barriers in your path may be genuine, even if they are not helpful. For any number of reasons, they aren't ready to embrace change. In reality, they can't help but transfer their own fear to you.

What can you do? Affirm that it's *not about you*. Criticism leveled at your efforts toward change provides information about their own fear and inadequacy. But it doesn't end there. Know this: Their criticism reveals insight about *them*; your response to criticism exposes some of your deepest beliefs about *you*.

Change triggers great challenges, but it also opens the door to great opportunities for personal growth. As you enter into a new territory, anticipate the criticism, learn to neutralize the naysayers in your life, and seize the opportunity to look within and refine your leadership identity.

REFLECT AND RESPOND

1. Think of a time when you were attempting to make a positive change in your life. Did you encounter personal resistance from others? Were you the target of any negative messages or attacks from naysayers?
2. To what extent have you personalized negative criticism?
3. As you ponder the range of emotions associated with change, how would you assess your ability to move past negative messages?
4. Have you ever felt threatened by another person's progress or achievement? Have you ever been a naysayer? How can you change that?

Remember This

If you plan to navigate the stormy seas of change, you must prepare for the inevitable attempts to discourage your progress and poison your plans. Leaders who are effective change agents learn not to personalize the negative reactions of others, even if they were intended to be personal attacks.

CHAPTER FIVE

NO ATTABOY TERRITORY
DEAFENING SILENCE

"There were strange sensory and psychological effects too. Scurvy seems to have disarmed the sensory inhibitors that keep taste, smell and hearing under control and stop us from feeling too much...This susceptibility of the senses was accompanied by a disposition to cry at the slightest disappointment, and to yearn hopelessly and passionately for home."

-Jonathan Lamb, *Captain Cook and the Scourge of Scurby*

THE REALITY OF CHANGE

Shift Your Focus

Personal or organizational change ushers in a flood of emotions and experiences. Your progress has awakened the criticism of others, which is why this phase of change is named the No Attaboy Territory. Yes, you crave affirmation. And at this juncture, you need support. Indeed, the scarcity of encouragement is glaring.

Remember, you're not the only person to make your way through this passage, even though it can feel like a sailor whose ship is stuck in the doldrums. In reality, that's far from what's happening. You're not enduring a period of inactivity; you're navigating the unexpected impact of change.

If you are able to tune out the noise from the outside, you can gain focus and clarity on what's happening on the inside. This is where dynamic agents of change begin the hard work of becoming a transformational force for change. This is real leadership transformation and where great leaders are born.

Educational research has made headway in the area of learning, which requires more than excellent content or inspiring delivery. Think about your greatest life lessons. When did it pierce through the ordinary and capture your heart and mind? What was the contextual fabric of the situation? It's inspiring to engage in discussions about learning styles, learning environments, and learning opportunities. But real learning revolves around a simple truth. In life, some of the most poignant lessons are learned in the midst of intense times of questioning. Simple questions take us on a journey of inspection and introspection. They include: *Why? Who am I? Where am I going? Can I make it?*

Ask Questions

Questions lead to learning. When you reach the point of having made a serious commitment to change and you're in the midst of it, you'll discover an unparalleled opportunity for serious questioning. Critical inquiry can take you down a powerful path of learning, and the No Attaboy Territory is a perfect place to engage. Beware! Change travelers who traverse this territory always face formidable challenges. The greatest victories in life are never won without a battle.

In the midst of change, learn to tune out the bad messages and find a place of quiet reflection. Actually, find ways to harness the value of messages you have tuned out in your past. The No Attaboy Territory can function as a crucible to refine your thought processes and your mental models. Ironically, once you tune out the noise, you can find a strange comfort in the moment as a new door opens for growth.

To tap into the value of the moment, focus on these two significant questions:

- "How do I handle information/messages?"
- "What am I learning about myself?"

How Do You Handle Information?

Can you remember a time when it was possible to avoid people? If you didn't want to see someone, you might hide. Not long ago, if you didn't want to talk to someone, you simply didn't answer your phone. It may have been twice as hard if you had a work phone and a home phone. Yes, bad news messages have been around for ages; however, the number of vehicles that carry these messages has grown exponentially. The messages *do not stop to rest.*

How do you handle these negative messages? The best leaders don't reject information simply because it's painful or uncomfortable. They have a process to weigh its value. The best decisions require openness to assessment, feedback, and information. Effective decision-making necessitates a filter. To receive what you need and reject the unfruitful noise around you, you want to focus on the commitment you made to change inside *you*. It begins with an honest confession such as this: *Acknowledge that information cannot affect your personal value and identity.*

Know this: "No matter where you go, there you are." This phrase might sound humorous, but it rings true. You need to get comfortable with the inner person making the journey through life with you. So find time for self-talk and ask, "What does the conversation inside my head reveal about me?" At this point in your journey, it's likely you'll be reviewing the hurtful words hurled at you by a naysayer or two. In addition, you may reflect on your own past experiences and even conduct a simple checklist with these questions: "Can I make it? What was I thinking? Do I have what it takes?"

Poor self-image is among the most powerful drivers of our actions and inner thoughts. Countless studies over time have shown that all people, at least in certain seasons of their lives, have struggled with their own sense of self-worth. That's why change functions as a crucible; it tends to cause things to bubble up to the surface. Accept that your change journey is often a crisis experience that encompasses your self-beliefs and self-doubts.

Hyper-connected World and Feelings of Inadequacy

An unintended consequence of living in a hyper-connected world can be a sense of overwhelming inadequacy. More than half a century ago, futurist Alvin Toffler saw this kind of world coming. In his classic book *Future Shock*, Toffler accurately predicted that, as the place of technology in our society increases, people's own sense of self-worth would decrease. He also predicted that a technology-driven culture would produce an age of lessened intimacy, increased pace of living, and the rise of unyielding stress. He was one of the first to predict the emergence of a kind of "pedal to the metal" living in which enough would never be enough. Along with that comes the hopeless feeling of "the more we try, the further we feel left behind." This ongoing effort to keep up ultimately could lead to a diminished sense of self—a pervasive conclusion that "I am not good enough."[3]

Today, we live at a faster pace than ever. There's even a clever acronym to describe our world. Leaders talk about "VUCA" as a shorthand expression of the pressures of Volatility, Uncertainty, Complexity, and Ambiguity. These concerns aren't relegated to a few alarmists. They affect everyone. How do these four conditions affect your life? Does your immediate context signal personal paralysis or opportunity?

The answers depend on your ability to filter and focus. To be sure, there is less time for the distractions from naysayers. But you can't afford to shut down and tune out information that can help you in your journey. Filtering information through your belief system will make the difference.

Do You Feel Good Enough?

If you dare to be vulnerable, you will confess having the familiar feeling that you are not good enough. It may be a fleeting thought or it may settle over you like a dark cloud. When your momentum toward your personal change vision stalls, questions of doubt can seize your focus. That's when your passage through the No Attaboy Territory can turn perilous or providential.

The ability of having a low level of self-belief toward being destructive cannot be understated. Ultimately, an inadequate self-portrait can lead

---

[3] Alvin Toffler. *Future Shock*. Bantam. 1984.

you to conclude that your value as a person will not come from simply you being you! Incorrectly, you may assume that your value doesn't come from your innate self-dignity or that you were created with such marvelous complexity in a world of billions. *You are the only one of you in the world.*

However, having a poor self-belief system discards this with remarks such as these: "I don't really matter! I'll never measure up! I made a mistake, and so I *am* a mistake." The most painful messages from naysayers on the shore can stick in your heart like a knife. They will resonate with your self-doubt if you give them room.

The impact of feeling inadequate as a human leads to a sense of shame and saying, "My meaning as an individual will not come from my being, since my being isn't good enough." Because each person was born with an innate quest for meaning—for a life that matters and for the desire to make a positive impact on our world—we desperately search elsewhere for a way to find our meaningful value as persons.

If your own *being* cannot be the source of your self-value, then it can only come from *doing*. If you cannot find meaning in the "who" you are, then it must come from "what" you achieve or earn. If it doesn't come from the inside, then it must come from the outside through your performance and specifically through how others judge that performance. As they do, they are, in your mind, directly judging your worth as a person. This is what it means to be a performance-based person.

Performance-Based Values Produce a Fear of Failure

You have launched into change with a strong commitment and motivation. You have a plan for execution. Your change experience has brought you far. So why are you having second thoughts? It's like that tinge of "buyer's remorse" as you drive away from the car dealership. What have you done? Will you turn back?

But when you consider reversing a deep personal change, it's not the same as taking advantage of a 24-hour return policy. The ramifications of a U-turn in the No Attaboy Territory are lasting. You realize that if you go back:

- You refute the internal messages that brought you forward.
- You give in to a different definition of yourself.
- You cast aside your leadership identity that believes change is possible.
- You discredit the beliefs that brought you to this point.

It sounds costly because it is. How does such a dramatic reversal take place? Consider it a disease that has many strains and mutations, but its core malady is this: *You insidiously think your identity is based on performance and the affirmation of others.* This disease can chronically drain your effectiveness. And you may think it has been eradicated, only to have it flare up again.

Leaders are especially susceptible to this malady during times of critical change. If you base your value as a leader on the changing tide of opinions rather than your deeply held beliefs and values, you'll find it difficult to sustain positive change. Said another way, if affirmation from others drives your determination, then you'll never make it through the No Attaboy Territory of change.

Terror of Failing

A performance-led self-valuing process leads to the terror of failing, which is how a fear of failure becomes a self-fulfilling prophecy. If your identity is balanced perilously on whether your present endeavor succeeds in the eyes of others, the stakes are high. At the first sign of disapproval, you will question whether the risk is worthwhile. But what could be worth sending a message to yourself and others that your life and leadership is a failure? This is why crossing the line of commitment can be a terrifying option. It's also why many begin a specific change only to quit before completing it.

Crossing the line of commitment invites inherent risk. It's not playing things safe; rather, it involves taking on a heightened level of uncertainty as well as exhilaration. In response to this deep fear of failing, the vast majority of people will opt not to cross the line of commitment. Know this: Crossing that line can quiet the deep, ongoing self-messages of *not being good enough* and daring to think you can succeed.

Crossing the Line

Not only does a healthy dose of self-awareness equip you for your personal development, it helps you gain perspective on how to interpret negativity. When you commit to change, your action may well stir up drama and pain within others observing you. When you cross the line of commitment, you can influence others who have refused change to face their own shame. So rather than address it, most will choose to hide from self-examination and project their problems onto others.

You must remind yourself that crossing the line will simultaneously stir your emotions and the emotions of everyone witnessing your movement from the shore. Dynamic leadership reveals a stark, uncomfortable contrast compared to those who remain stagnant.

It's painful to witness another person's successful progress while remaining stuck in your own journey. Therefore, the easiest way to relieve the pain is to stop its source. Naysayers desperate for relief want you to "quit stirring things up in their souls" and "let sleeping dogs lie." This is why you will often receive impassioned advice from others trying to delay or deny your progress. At times, the advice turns to intentional sabotage. When people are deeply uncomfortable, they won't be neutral about finding comfort. In fact, they will require a deliberate, often intensive effort to regain their sense of comfort again. Such people are willing to violate your personal boundaries to express their dismay. They certainly aren't afraid to dive into your business, even at the risk of your disapproval, because they feel a deeper discomfort they're trying to silence.

While these people may couch their efforts in terms of a deep concern for *you*, it's actually about *them*.

Only You Can Stop the Journey

Can naysayers stop change? (Recall the discussion about victim thinking. At this stage in the change process, take time to review the importance of rejecting victim thinking in Chapter One.) Despite the challenges you face, this is *not* the time to give in to self-pity. As you take responsibility for where you are, you will resist the undertow that will drag you down.

Do not resign. Remember, you control how much power you give to the words spoken by naysayers. You control whether you continue toward your vision of change or not. When you take responsibility for your life and your leadership, you are prepared to consider the consequences of your decisions. So before you turn around, count the costs in these two ways.

THE COSTS OF TURNING AROUND

1. If you turn around, you will diminish your willingness to take risks, experience change, and lead change in the future.

2. If you choose to focus on the messages of the naysayers, you will waste valuable time and energy on destructive thoughts and actions.

1. **If you turn around, you will diminish your willingness to take risks, experience change, and lead change in the future.**

Here's an example. Bob has been with his company for more than twenty years. For most of that time, he was known as a vivacious, get-it-done leader whom others relied on heavily for insights and direction. He was also a source of vitality and energy for the company at large.

Sadly, over time Bob gained the nickname "Phone-it-in Bob." What happened? Five years ago, he was assigned to report to a new CFO who has a strong authoritarian leadership style. When Bob would propose a change or carry a recommendation forward, the CFO was quick to scrutinize and ask pointed questions. Bob took the CFO's aggressive stance as a sign of no confidence. Worse, he internalized the pushback as personal rejection and began to withdraw. That's when he commonly voiced the phrase to his peers, "The one who sticks his head up will have it chopped off." In meetings, he became known for telling his bosses only what he thought they wanted to hear. He never volunteered for an assignment; he'd only take it if his boss insisted.

CHAPTER FIVE

All of his teammates hated working with Phone-it-in Bob. They knew that, if he were leading their task group, it would never take any risk that might engender pushback from senior leaders. Bob didn't want to get on their "radar," as he liked to say. So the group would get enough done to escape unwanted attention but never excelled in achieving real change. Because Bob took any criticism of his recommendations personally, it had rendered him ineffective. He had lost the respect of his peers who understood his focus was on sliding toward retirement as quietly as possible.

Bob didn't just wake up one morning and decide to forfeit his leadership potential. Rather, it was a slow fade marked by a tendency to give away his power. Similarly, if we give credence to other people as authenticators of our self-worth and value, these painful negative reactions will prevent us from fulfilling responsibility to ourselves or others. Like Bob, we will cease to inspire others.

2. **If you focus on the messages of the naysayers, you will waste valuable time and energy on destructive thoughts and actions.**

   Personalizing the resistance from others redirects your focus in an unproductive manner. When criticism becomes personal, defensiveness abounds. That defensiveness restricts objectivity, and lost productivity results.

   How easily do you get lost in resentment over a perceived lack of support? How much time and mental energy do you invest vilifying others over and over in your mind? Beware. Instead of planning your next step toward your vision, you waste time planning your next response to your opposition. With each passing breath spent this way, you will forfeit time and energy that could be invested in overcoming real obstacles and moving toward your vision.

Here's an example. A 16,000-member Midwestern tribe developed and implemented a plan to advance economic vitality and opportunity for its people. One substantial portion of the plan called for constructing and operating a state-of-the-art alternative energy plant. The proposed plant would process 150 tons of trash daily and produce "green" electricity to power 4,000 homes. The plant's promise of revenue and jobs for tribe members generated a high level of enthusiasm.

The tribe's innovative plan relied on clean technology that had never been implemented on a commercial scale. Predictably, antagonism emerged from an adjacent city. While organizing a massive protest to stop the construction permit, the opposition focused attention on a lack of information regarding emissions and the impact on the environment. Reeling against the unanticipated outcry, the leaders of the project reacted defensively, even publicly, suggesting that racism was at the source of these "personal attacks against the tribe." They displayed a siege mentality against all opposition. Yet despite the heavy and continual opposition, tribe members completed all of the necessary federal and state permits during the following two years.

Early in the permit-gathering stage, the tribal government's office of environmental affairs conducted an analysis of the ongoing process and recommended that project leaders proactively respond to the criticism with additional research and data development. They concluded that, although the information and methods of delivery might be unpleasant to receive, the naysayers' concerns were legitimate.

Again, project leaders protested that their own environmental affairs leaders were deliberately sabotaging the energy project. So rather than proceeding with recommended action, they selected a new construction site in a city outside of the reservation to avoid being accountable to the tribal agency.

Following two subsequent years of posturing between opposing sides, the city council withdrew permission for the tribe to build within its boundaries. In effect, the city council agreed with the findings of the tribal government's office of environmental affairs. The council found that the tribe's project leaders had not responded to requests for more detailed information. Sadly, because project leaders personalized the earlier information, they wasted the opportunity to remedy the concerns. Because they did not see the concerns as "just information," they dug in and resisted, failing to address key causal factors.

Ultimately, reacting defensively to the messengers instead of acting on their message led to the failure of the once-promising project.

Are You Missing Valuable Information?

Great leaders learn to use critical words to their advantage by "detaching" from the emotion of the message. Personal detachment allows you to process information objectively. That means you'll be able to detach more successfully from an inappropriate emotion to harsh criticism when you understand *why* others might react with instinctive negativity to your constructive change efforts.

Whether you're engaged in personal or organizational change, you must learn to expect criticism and resist the temptation to personalize resistance. Only then will you be able to use information to your benefit. Doing this will enable you to regard resistance as neutral data rather than a critical judgment of you.

REFLECT AND RESPOND

1. What are your most powerful *positive* internal messages?
2. What are your most powerful *negative* internal messages?
3. To remind yourself of the positive, write down these messages and look at them every day for the next week.
4. Identify the fears associated with your negative internal messages, and then confront your fears with the positive messages you wrote.

Remember This

If you are able to tune out the noise from the outside, you can gain focus and clarity on what's happening on the inside. This is where great leaders are born.

CHAPTER SIX

KEEP THE ROWERS ROWING

"A bend in the road is not the end of the road unless you fail to make the turn."

-Helen Keller

THE REALITY OF CHANGE

What Happened to Todd's Dream?

For Todd, there was no looking back. He plunged into his dream of becoming a helicopter pilot. Within two years, he had completed his training to become an instrument-rated flyer. During this time, he juggled jobs, faced severe financial hardships, and worked tirelessly to care for his young family. In those early days, facing daunting student aid debt and weathering unending sacrifices, Todd nearly gave up his dream on many occasions. But he was determined.

Each milestone accomplished emboldened Todd to continue forward. He owned his dream. Once he completed the civilian flight training program, he set his sights on pursuing the best the U.S. Army had to offer. He declared his commitment to become a U.S. Army Blackhawk Helicopter Pilot.

Immediately, Todd was bombarded with resistance from almost all corners of his life. Some of his longtime friends laughed and told him his dream was unrealistic. They said he'd never make it for few who try ever succeed. Family members fretted for his safety and asked him to reconsider his choice. At the onset, only two people gave him positive reinforcement: his wife and his father. He called them his "champions."

On top of the deafening negative discord, he learned of the stringent requirement demanded of the position. Less than 10 percent of worthy applicants were accepted into the warrant officer program. Unfortunately, Todd didn't pass his initial flight physical due to poor eyesight. When he learned that surgery could correct his eye impairment, he borrowed money from his family to complete the procedure. But he would have to wait six months before he could retake the physical.

During this time, finding employment was an ongoing challenge. Few employers wanted to hire and train someone who might soon be leaving for the armed services. While waiting to retake his exam, he and his family moved into his parents' home, a difficult move for a proud man with a wife and young child.

After six months of tedious waiting, he completed a new exam. Then the army doctor informed Todd the surgery had been performed improperly. To have any chance of entering the flight program, more surgery was necessary. And even with the additional surgery, he couldn't guarantee success.

Predicting personal setbacks and anticipating the cost of delays is an inexact science. To a young man caught in limbo, the temptation to throw in the towel can loom large. Todd felt the palpable tension between perseverance and patience. Yet he reached deep and discovered the tenacity he needed to try one more time. The second surgical procedure meant he would incur further medical costs and six more months of placing his life on hold. Again, not everyone admired his courage. With negative comments swirling around his decision, maintaining sight of his dream became a daily struggle for Todd. It was difficult not to give into the discouraging words.

Before you learn whether Todd was successful or not, it's important to ask the obvious question, "Is it worth it to keep moving forward?" For Todd, it was. He kept rowing. Eventually, he was able to realize his dream as a pilot—a dream that expanded into many new adventures.

Will You Keep Rowing in Spite of the Pain?

Like Todd, you might experience a disheartening physical phenomenon. And as you grow older, you lose flexibility. Try to touch the floor without bending your knees. Is it more difficult than it used to be? Is there a prescription for recovering flexibility? You might do lots of stretching, but if you haven't stretched in a while, you'll notice some discomfort. There's a delicate balance between a healthy level of tension and any pain signaling you've likely hurt yourself.

When you're rowing, for example, the weather can change, the wind can shift, and competing voices among team members can amplify criticism. Know this: Although external challenges such as pain and weather are significant, every victory is won on the inside.

In *The Boys in the Boat*, Daniel James Brown gives a vivid description of the battle for focus when pain increases.

> And that is perhaps the first and most fundamental thing that all novice oarsmen must learn about competitive rowing in the upper echelons of the sport: that pain is part and parcel of the deal. It's not a question of whether you will hurt, or of how much you will hurt; it's a question of what you will do, and how well you will do it, while pain has her wanton way with you.[4]

Painful perseverance is part of The Reality of Change. It's not a question of whether you will feel the burn but whether you will keep pressing forward. You'll never be able to engage and continue the process of personal transformation without a measure of discomfort. Will you keep rowing in spite of the pain?

It's time to learn how to sustain change, to develop endurance. Endurance combines your ability to anticipate and embrace the tension that leads to greater flexibility while learning to protect yourself from unnecessary pain

---

[4] From *The Boys in the Boat* copyright © 2013 by Daniel James Brown. Reprinted by permission of Penguin Books, New York.

that shuts down positive change. Sustaining positive change is rewarding; it's also arduous. To achieve it requires pushing aside the self-inflicted pain associated with faulty belief systems and drawing strength from deeper, stronger, more virtuous truths. These will fuel your endurance.

The Value of Endurance

"Never give in. Never give in. Never, never, never, never—in nothing, great or small, large or petty—never give in, except to convictions of honor and good sense. Never yield to force. Never yield to the apparently overwhelming might of the enemy."

- Sir Winston Churchill

To persevere and continue changing in a positive direction requires being willing to continue your efforts beyond the point of initial fatigue or frustration. You already know the drive to endure won't come from the positive affirmation of others. Certainly hearing encouraging words will help you on your journey, but there's no such thing as vicarious endurance. Rather, it comes from within.

The best way to acquire endurance is to invest in it before you need it. You do that through clarity, heart, and mindfulness. To the oarsmen in a racing shell, it's what Brown described as "M-I-B"—keeping your mind in the boat:

Morry shouted, "M-I-B, M-I-B, M-I-B!" over and over to the rhythm of their stroke. The initialism stood for "mind in boat." It was meant as a reminder that from the time an oarsman steps into a racing shell until the moment that the boat crosses the finish line, he must keep his mind focused on what is happening inside the boat. His whole world must shrink down to the small space within the gunwales. He must maintain a singular focus on the rower just ahead of him and the voice of the coxswain calling out commands. [5]

THREE INVESTMENTS THAT YIELD ENDURANCE

1. Clarity - Determine what is most important in your life.
2. Heart - Live by what captures your heart.
3. Mindfulness - Increase your awareness.

---

1. Clarity – What's Most Important in Your Life?

Endurance is part desire and part fortitude. Mostly it reveals what lies within you—your true character. There's no substitute for a clear resolve to continue to march forward. It sounds cliché, but you will have to reach inside yourself to persist on achieving new levels of personal leadership.

For some people, reaching deep inside is like buying a piece of property you've never seen. To draw strength from within means taking time to ponder your existence and answering big questions about your life such as: *What is most important to you? What is not important to you? What is your purpose?*

The quest for identity can seem like a relentless march. Yet, it's precisely during the march that you will strengthen your resolve.

Endurance flourishes when you're attached to something bigger than

---

[5] Ibid

the moment. If you lack a clear sense of purpose, you will also lack the necessary resources for the long haul. How can you gain a long-term perspective about what matters? By developing a personal vision based on what's most important in your life.

Regard your personal vision as a tangible expression of your priorities. Having a clear vision statement will help produce endurance in a couple of ways. First, it helps because your vision remains unaffected by circumstances; it acts as a combination of compass and anchor. As such, it will yield directional guidance and personal stability—essential elements when you're cutting through the waves of uncertainty. Turbulence on the outside can cause a great deal of discomfort, but it cannot threaten your identity. Having stability on the inside always combats instability on the outside.

Second, your personal vision statement will fortify your identity, which is your best defense against personal attacks. Remember, if you don't know who you really are, you'll be subject to a barrage of messages but won't be able to filter internal and external messages that are untrue. It's possible criticism will eat away at your stamina.

On the other hand, when you know who you are, you can quickly insulate your identity from destructive information. Your personal vision statement becomes a powerful prescription for endurance.

2. Heart – What Captures Your Heart?

Conversations in the business world about vision statements and core values are as common as talk about the weather. No one would dare argue against the importance of either the weather or core values. But even though conversations about core values have multiplied, they don't necessarily translate into recognizable behaviors. Focus on your personal *vision*, which reinforces your identity. And focus on your *values*, which provide necessary boundaries for how you live out your identity.

Know this: Both vision and values find traction when they capture your heart as well as your mind.

Core values reside within, but they cannot survive if they remain hidden inside. Real, heartfelt values must render action that reinforces the message and meaning of those values. Because your heart is the center of your being, until values capture your heart, they aren't attached to your core. It's far too easy to use the word "core" and magically pretend that values have greater depth. *However, they are not core values until they are integrated into your life.* And like the buoys keeping you in the safe channel, it's those values that produce endurance. If you ignore your core values, a shipwreck could be imminent.

You might have to go back to the drawing board, for only by living your values can you sustain your efforts and contribute to endurance. Not only will this prevent disaster but your core values will also guide your movement efficiently. And when your behavior aligns with your values, you don't waste energy.

In contrast, a lack of alignment creates unnecessary friction that drags on your energy and momentum. Be assured that your most efficient movement will always be guided by your core *values*, and your personal *vision* based on core values will illuminate an intentional path forward.

3. **Mindfulness – How Can You Increase Awareness?**

Distractions in life abound. The buoys in the water are only helpful when you can see them. Therefore, what you choose to notice is extraordinarily important. When you allow something to disturb, affect, or shake your world, you open a gateway to your attitude and redirect the course of your life. And yet, you can find the beauty in everyday events. Sometimes it's simply a willingness to pause and inhale the fresh wind that surrounds you.

Describing mindfulness can be fun and begins with asking these questions: *What do you see? What do you feel? What do you hear?* Now consider two levels of awareness. First is mindfulness that accompanies exhilaration. Imagine something that awakens your senses—the smell of the ocean, the sound of a sail capturing the wind, the sensation of movement, the refreshing mist on your face as you break through the surface of ocean. Your heart beats and you embrace the moment. Finding this kind of mindfulness invigorating, you feel fully alive.

However, if that's your only impression of what it means to be mindful, you're missing a great deal.

The second level of mindfulness is a cultivated sensitivity to your thoughts, your feelings, and what's happening beneath your exterior. It comes from within. Few leaders pay enough attention to this because it takes time, requires quiet, and thrives when being still. Only through careful examination of what's happening *inside* will you be able to see the *outside* as you should.

The more self-aware you are, the more mindful you will be of your surroundings. When you're the only one who understands the meaning of the moment, such mindfulness can produce a rush of energy that accompanies success. The real power of mindfulness comes through a cultivated awareness of everyday reality. It can unleash a new level of authenticity. Authentic leaders find extraordinary beauty in the ordinary, and it nourishes them. For them, every day provides an occasion to learn.

THE REALITY OF CHANGE

When you realize that *every day* is intensely valuable, leadership development opportunities become unlimited. All of life becomes a practice field for learning. Ask athletes to list the potential benefits of practice and they'll include a time to train, a time to learn discipline, and a safe place to make mistakes and learn how to avoid repeating them. Practice is about stretching, pushing, receiving coaching, and developing stamina. And, yes, practice is about building endurance.

What if you found a way to tap into this treasure of mindfulness every day? You will transform your journey of change into a productive and fulfilling practice field. Your identity will be refined and your core values tested. Through this practice of mindfulness, you will endure and emerge a better person.

REFLECT AND RESPOND

1. **Clarity** – What are the five most important qualities of your character?
2. **Heart** – What are your "non-negotiables" in life? Ask a trusted friend to describe what you value most.
3. **Mindfulness** – Commit time to be quiet. Be still. Is it difficult to unplug? Why? Write down what you thought about when you were quiet.

Remember This

Endurance is required. To persevere and continue the change, you must be willing to continue your efforts to change beyond the point of initial fatigue or frustration.

THE REALITY OF CHANGE

PART THREE:
THE DESTINATION

"Human beings are works in progress that
mistakenly think they are finished."

-Dan Gilbert

THE REALITY OF CHANGE

CHAPTER SEVEN

THE POWER OF A CLEAR PURPOSE
SEE IT BEFORE YOU ARRIVE

"Panic causes tunnel vision. Calm acceptance of danger allows
us to more easily assess the situation and see the options."

-Simon Sinek

THE REALITY OF CHANGE

Can You See It?

Seeing is believing. Believing is seeing. Do you see? Do you believe? Vision is powerful. When you can see the destination ahead of time, it draws you to it. When you visualize success, you will naturally lean forward. A real vision provides the fuel for the journey. With vision, hope is renewed and resiliency increases. You're encouraged to keep your vision alive at all costs.

Because the best defense is a great offense, use your vibrant vision as your offense. It will be your best bet to defend against the evil twins known as fear and doubt. By now, you understand how and why this malevolent duo frequently wreaks havoc on change. They attack positive change like a mutating virus that starts small and spreads quickly. By the time the symptoms are full blown, you have lost your joy, your relationships suffer, and paralysis sets in. But of all the debilitating effects, blindness is the worst. Nothing hinders your progress like the inability to see your way forward. Fear and doubt cloud your vision, reduce visibility, and stymie your progress.

If you cannot see your way forward, it's hard to believe you will make it. Vision will keep these treacherous threats at bay.

Keeping Vision Alive

There's a tendency to focus on the initial surge of enthusiasm derived from envisioning a plan, to moving from the current reality to a preferred future. But the first taste of a better tomorrow can be fleeting. Be sure you understand the best practices for sharing and sustaining movement over time. Many change initiatives begin with a compelling vision. Like a powerful catalyst, the vision inspires movement forward. But it's natural for a vision to fade. It's even more challenging to intensify the vision over time. The great leaders have learned how.

THREE WAYS TO SUSTAIN A ROBUST VISION

1. Health - Invest in your physical, emotional, and spiritual health.
2. Focus - Define what is most important and fix your attention there.
3. Heroes - Listen, learn and follow the best examples.

1. Health – Invest in your physical, emotional, and spiritual health.

When you think of health, think of nutrition. When you think of a strong, vibrant, and healthy vision, think of nourishment. A vision does *not* exist in isolation. Every vision is born and resides in the heart, soul, and mind of a person. Behind every healthy vision is a healthy leader. That means for your vision to thrive (let alone survive), you need to guard your physical, emotional, and spiritual health.

Here's an example. Greg and Marcia were gifted and highly respected professionals. Successful in their careers, they enjoyed a wonderful family life with two children. Both earned a Ph.D. in their given fields of study, having proven they had what it takes to persevere. Yet even though they had a history of influencing their professional disciplines, the institutions they served, and their communities, both Greg and Marcia reached a point in life of debilitating struggle.

Specifically, one of their children was diagnosed with an illness that left her in constant pain and chronically fatigued. As caring parents, their attention focused toward finding a diagnosis and solution for their daughter's ailment. In a relentless quest to aid her healing, they had traveled the country, spending months at a time in various treatment centers. They felt exhausted and discouraged as their daughter showed minimal progress despite their ceaseless efforts. Both Greg and Marcia exhibited signs of depression, struggling to maintain a semblance of family while often split apart as their daughter completed treatment programs with only her mother at her side.

Throughout their ordeal, many well-meaning people had given them the "work on your attitude and stay positive" speech. Others had attempted to support them by providing "how to" lists—as if easy formulas worked magic for their situation. (As you know, easy answers rarely work in complex life situations.)

Marcia had set aside her career and was at her wit's end. Greg struggled from low energy, a lack of focus, and a sense of hopelessness. Quietly, they confided they felt trapped in a deep hole with no way out. Their desperation had pushed them to the point of surrender.

Intervention came from a trusted friend who asked these pointed questions: "Why don't you stop trying? What hinders you from giving up on life?" They both recited a litany of reasons why quitting was *not* an option by giving compelling reasons beyond caring for their daughter. The reasons included being involved in people's lives and providing a lasting contribution to curing diseases and advancing wellness in others.

After stating that aloud to their friend, the fog slowly cleared so they could recognize what had happened. Over time, little by little, they recognized how their hope had eroded. A mixture of fatigue, mental anguish, and anger had siphoned their energy. Their sense of hopelessness coincided with a growing disconnect with the world outside of their predicament. In providing care for their daughter, they'd unwittingly failed to nourish themselves. That led to withdrawing into a cocoon of despair and losing sight of anything beyond the crisis.

Real change began with this realization. While continuing to care for their daughter, they found ways to reconnect with whatever brought renewal and depth to their lives. Several weeks after this realization, both experienced a transformation in terms of regained energy and a sense of renewed hope in their lives. They learned to reengage with others. Even with disorder, they realized, they could still feel contentment by reengaging their purpose.

About the same time, Marcia and Greg saw an improvement in their other daughter's overall disposition, activity, and energy. They had transferred the same insights to her, and she displayed a greater effort to help with her sister's needs and do activities to aid others. She, too, was learning life could be worthwhile despite ongoing uncertainty. In being true to their purpose, these parents found new ways to give to their daughters, to each other, to others, and to themselves.

There is a reason the two words "balanced" and "nutrition" appear together so frequently. As humans, we have a need for balance. During times of crisis, we need inner strength to sustain our vision and continue to develop. That's when it's tempting to abandon the very things that provide us with health.

2. **Focus – Define what is most important and fix your attention there.**

Every day you live, you will focus on various things. It can be your vision or it can be the loudest noise. Frequently, the loudest noise is a negative one that threatens, dilutes, and distracts. If your vision is fading, you've likely drifted off course and allowed distance to separate you from your vision. In a world where hyper-connectivity has become the norm, it's important to guard against the detrimental effects of information overload.

How much information do you ingest that does little to encourage your movement toward your vision? How much energy do you invest in distractions that work against positive change in your life? As you answer these questions, recall the keys to endurance from Chapter Six—that is, *clarify* what is most important, *live* by what captures your heart, and *increase* your mindfulness. Each of these can lead to greater focus and an enduring vision.

3. **Heroes – Listen, learn, and follow the best examples.**

Having a vision implies that leadership is all about sight, but it's also about hearing. In the journey of change, something magnificent happens as you near the vision. The din of the naysayers begins to fade. A new set of voices can be discerned—ones from those who have experienced successful change. Heroes are not perfect; their lessons extend from their humanness. It's always tempting to dehumanize heroes, to pretend they didn't have to work as hard or face the same challenges as you. But The Reality of Change challenges everyone, even heroes. That's why it's important to listen, to learn, and to aspire to create positive change.

Vision and Change, Change and Vision

The relationship between vision and change is symbiotic. Vision enables change; change provides focus and fine-tuning for your vision. When you overcome the obstacles to personal change, you climb to a new vista where your outlook is different. This new outlook enables you to lift your head and dare to look into the future. You no longer live in The Land of Status Quo. You have resolved to persevere. You keep on rowing.

Because you have bolstered your belief system, your perspective has changed. Vision isn't reserved for dreamers; it's your greatest ally. Let it become *your* story, the narrative of your life.

REFLECT AND RESPOND

1. **Health**
   - How are you investing in your physical health?
   - How are you investing in your emotional health?
   - How are you investing in your spiritual health?
2. **Focus**
   - Is your vision clear? Clarify your vision and identify the greatest threats to your focus.
3. **Heroes**
   - Make a list of your heroes. Identify at least one admirable trait in each hero.

Remember This

The relationship between vision and change is symbiotic. Vision enables change. Change provides focus and fine-tuning for your vision.

THE REALITY OF CHANGE

CHAPTER EIGHT

THE LAND OF POSITIVE RESULTS
THE AMAZING IMPACT OF REAL CHANGE

"We are products of our past but we don't have to be prisoners of it."

-Rick Warren

THE REALITY OF CHANGE

What Would You Do If You Weren't Afraid?

Seth is a precocious little boy who refuses to believe that life should be contained. He spends his days soaking up experiences and sharing the aftereffects as he navigates life with the passion and personality of a golden retriever puppy. So when Seth bursts into a room, he delivers messages to anyone who will listen. One day, this message exploded from his being like a carbonated drink from a shaken bottle: "I jumped off the high dive!"

Now, put yourself in the room with Seth and ponder your reactions to this message. *What do you remember?* Perhaps your first response was a vivid flashback to your childhood. You see yourself climbing the ladder rung by rung at a community pool. Slowly and methodically, you march toward the end of the board. It's your first time jumping!

Your imagination becomes a portal and you are in character. In your mind, you become an Olympic athlete or a pirate forced to walk the plank. Inside your gut is a mixture of fear, anticipation, determination, and a newfound appreciation for social awareness. *Who is watching? Can I? Will I? What if? What's the worst thing that could happen?*

Pay attention to the emotions you've resurrected from your memory. They are important. *Do you smile?* You're able to listen to Seth and laugh, smile, and enjoy the moment. The smile of a child is magnetic, contagious. It evokes warmth and sincerity that's irresistible.

What would you say to Seth? Push aside your concerns and search for the best congratulatory words you can find. Celebrate with him. This is a monumental accomplishment.

Were you inspired? Was Seth a hero in your eyes? Jumping off a high diving board is a formidable challenge for a child. It's easy to look for heroes in all the wrong places, idolizing certain aspects of success while missing out on everyday shows of inspiration. That's why, for the moment, this brave little man is your hero.

Having experienced The Reality of Change, Seth has found his voice.

Freedom to Soar

The Reality of Change provides a different kind of platform within which resides transformational leadership. This is your new address. No longer do you call The Land of Status Quo home. You live in The Land of Positive Results.

When you consider the positive benefits of change, do not limit your results to the obvious. The trajectory of personal change stretches beyond the immediate dividends of an accomplished goal. *Positive change helps you find your voice that metaphorically describes the message and meaning of your leadership.* It endows your voice with three distinct and valuable qualities. First and foremost, your voice will resonate with a newfound freedom. Second, it endows you with courage. Finally, it allows you to lead from a higher level.

Once you have faced your fears and emerged a victor, you will discover freedom. It's not as though you'll never face fear again. Yet, you have experienced breaking free from the chains that kept you from discovering a greater potential. You have tasted new freedom and whetted your appetite for exploration. Experience has taught you that your best leadership lies beyond your comfort zone. Before this journey, your view was limited by your own beliefs and biases. You couldn't see beyond your fears. Now that you have successfully confronted those fears, you are free to be authentic, free to dream, free to soar.

THE REALITY OF CHANGE

Courage to Choose What is Best

Deep change is an arduous path that engages the total person—the heart, mind, and body. The best choices in life require courage as defined this way: "Mental or moral strength to venture, persevere, and withstand danger, fear, or difficulty." The English word for "courage" is derived from the Latin word *cor* and the Anglo-French word *coer*, which means heart.

Change touches the heart. Courage springs from the heart. Leaders who possess the mettle to choose what is *best* ahead of what is *easiest* understand what it means to lead with heart. Courage gives your voice depth.

Opportunity to Lead at a Higher Level

Inspiring leadership comes from those who have a track record of freedom, courage, and willingness to lead. Change is an exercise in self-leadership, but it cannot end with the self. Although self-leadership is essential, *selfish* leadership is a waste of talent. It must be shared.

Positive change weaves the past with the future, and it connects people with each other. As you gain a greater appreciation for those who have traveled before you, your perspective will grow. You embrace the opportunity to influence those who will follow as you steward your freedom, courage, and investment in others. That becomes your legacy.

Change begins with you, but it's never only about you. Your leadership legacy is about you *and* your investment in others. When you take the safe route at the proverbial fork in the road, you will forfeit an untold number of opportunities to inspire others. Initially, your vision may have been limited to your own concerns. But with every successful journey, you open up a panoramic view of potential relationships. You will be able to see further and view The Reality of Change through a broader lens.

Know this: Great leaders never stop learning, growing, and touching the lives of those around them.

LEADING CHANGE

1. Provides real-time opportunities to develop others.
2. Provides unique mentoring experiences.
3. Yields unparalleled teachable moments.

Jake's Story

Jake climbed aboard a plane and settled in for a transatlantic flight. Between a few naps, he rehearsed his speech in his mind. In a few days, he would be presenting a commencement address to a graduating class of young leaders. After delivering the address, he planned to engage with a large group of leaders for a series of talks on leadership. Cross-cultural speaking always produced a mixture of nerves and excitement for him.

The series of lectures Jake had planned would provide an overview of emerging leadership issues. He chose topics that were applicable yet safe. But upon his arrival, Jake's host revealed a number of conflict situations among those in the group he was addressing. For one, significant jealousy had arisen among them. The host made an impassioned plea for Jake to facilitate a meeting among the leaders regarding these issues. As a result, he faced a clear-cut decision to stay in his comfort zone and play it safe or get the leaders involved in a meaningful discussion. Would Jake cast aside the lectures he had prepared and dive into sensitive subjects, address the conflicts, and share in dialogue about future leadership opportunities?

THE REALITY OF CHANGE

Jake did set aside his plans and engaged the leaders in an authentic conversation about leadership. Knowing the sensitive issues were fraught with danger and uncertainty, he still chose to step out of his comfort zone. He recognized that this occasion presented a real-life opportunity to make a difference. It was a risk. It was a change.

After the week was over, Jake felt relieved and even rejuvenated by the experience. He was transparent during the process, yet deeply engaged in the real issues of the moment. His authenticity translated into a rich experience for the participants and a life lesson for Jake. This lesson applies to you, too. When it comes to engaging in positive change, it's important to remind yourself of both the internal and external rewards of leaving your comfort zone and serving others.

Risks and Rewards

Risks are worth it. Change is rewarding. This is The Reality of Change. And going to The Land of Positive Results provides exciting opportunities for personal stewardship. With these opportunities, you have enormous potential and a wealth of experience and knowledge.

Fear of change can become a locked safe. Within it, you lock up your resources, dreams, and opportunities to keep them guarded against danger and risk. Now you know how to crack open the safe; you already possess the combination. When you release your fears, you are free to invest in your future and the future of others.

REFLECT AND RESPOND

Write your legacy statement here:

I wish to be remembered for_____

_____

_____.

Remember This

The trajectory of personal change stretches beyond the immediate reward of achieving your goal. Change helps you find your voice, which metaphorically describes the message and meaning of your leadership.

THE REALITY OF CHANGE

POSTSCRIPT
BEWARE THE NEW LAND OF STATUS QUO

BEWARE THE NEW LAND
OF STATUS QUO

"Nothing fails like success. It freezes you in patterns that brought you
success twelve months before but that will bring you failure today."

-Leonard Sweet

THE REALITY OF CHANGE

Change. Something wonderful and terrible has just happened.

You have arrived at your destination. That's wonderful. But there's a major gravitational pull to settle in and create a new comfort zone. That's terrible.

What happens next depends on your desire to keep your legs fresh. Also, during the excitement of change, it's easy to fall prey to a clever trap. Your identity can become wrapped up in the change. Despite your effort to fuel your change with a robust vision and secure identity, the energetic pace of change can leave you a little unsettled. The remedy will be to "settle" into a new norm. *How will you resist the temptation to get "stuck" in a new comfort zone? How will you apply change as a catalyst for continued personal growth?*

CHANGE IS A CATALYST FOR CONTINUED DEVELOPMENT

1. Now that your eyes are open to change, use them to scan the horizon for opportunities.
2. Your experiences are worth sharing. Seize opportunities to inspire and teach others.
3. Revisit your dreams often and write them down.

Your Legacy

The danger of a "new norm" is the settling part, but you don't have to settle. The Reality of Change opens the door for lifelong learning and transformation. Once you have successfully traversed this sea of change, you will awaken to greater opportunities. You can and should continue to stretch and grow and increase positive influence.

POSTSCRIPT

Remember, your personal transformation is never only about you. Investing in others will prevent stagnation. Your experiences prepare you to enrich your community, improve your organization, and engage in relationships with greater transparency and fulfillment. You are an agent of change. You have a legacy to leave.

***

"I have walked that long road to freedom. I have tried not to falter; I have made missteps along the way. But I have discovered the secret that after climbing a great hill, one only finds that there are many more hills to climb. I have taken a moment here to rest, to steal a view of the glorious vista that surrounds me, to look back on the distance I have come. But I can only rest for a moment, for with freedom comes responsibilities, and I dare not linger, for my long walk is not ended."

-Nelson Mandela

THE REALITY OF CHANGE

ABOUT INITIATIVEONE

InitiativeOne transforms leaders and their organizations, helping them foster high-performing work cultures defined by authenticity, transparency, safe environments, and deep respect.

THE REALITY OF CHANGE

InitiativeOne, founded in 1999, is dedicated to facilitating accelerated, positive change in leaders and organizations. Its proprietary processes are customized for each client and focus on improving the behaviors of key leaders—how they function, how they behave, how they make decisions, and how they are viewed by others within the organization.

Under the direction and commitment of its founder, Dr. Fred Johnson, InitiativeOne has engaged with a diverse group of clients—from small businesses with fewer than 20 employees to multinational corporations employing over 100,000 people. Clients include United States Steel, Honeywell, Caterpillar, GEA Farm Technologies, McDonnell Douglas Aerospace, McDonald's (franchise owners), Whirlpool, Continental Homes, Macerich, Westcor, Realty Executives International, Transamerica, Compass Bank, Banner Health, Unison Health Plan, Seattle Seahawks' and Green Bay Packers' coaching staffs.

The iOne Transformation Process

Leaders lead by example. When key leaders make a commitment to, and consistently model, desired leadership behaviors, your entire organization will achieve greater success. You will see verifiable results in morale, productivity, efficiency, and profitability.

When you are ready to truly transform your organization, we come to you! Our leadership transformation process begins with Discovery. We identify the organizational challenges and core issues specific to you and your leadership team.

The InitiativeOne proprietary processes underscore behaviors, thinking, and attitudes. Its time-tested design is based on published business case studies and evidence-based leadership principles. We meet with your team for three hours a week for nine weeks. We will challenge your key leaders to define and improve their positive behaviors . . . leading to open, transparent communication, positive accountability, and effective decision making. This results in eliminating negative energy and fear within your organization, and creates new paths for enhanced productivity and exceptional results.

Results You Can Expect from Vision-Driven Leaders:

- Improved perspective and decision making
- Increased capacity to relate and communicate
- Heightened creativity and innovation
- Improved accountability to self and others
- Higher levels of confidence and performance
- Reduced anxiety, stress, and conflict

Website: http://www.initiative-one.com
Email: info@initiative-one.com

Leadership and Organizational Transformation, Executive Coaching, Executive Retreats, Leadership Keynote Speaking, University Leadership Curriculum

THE REALITY OF CHANGE

ABOUT THE AUTHORS

DR. FRED JOHNSON is the results-oriented founder and CEO of InitiativeOne, Institute of Business Leadership. Founded in 1999, InitiativeOne is a leadership firm that develops an organization's most important and only sustainable resource, its people. He and his staff inspire cultural change within an organization by focusing on improved behaviors of the organization's key leaders.

While pastoring four churches for nearly two decades, Dr. Johnson developed a proprietary model demonstrating a pattern of how people respond to change, both positively and negatively. After training pastors to be more effective leaders, word soon spread to corporate leaders, and he began to address their leadership teams on how to effectively lead positive change.

Today, Dr. Johnson is a highly sought-after speaker and a nationally recognized expert on the implications of different generations working together. He has taught his leadership and organizational process to groups as diverse as senior executives of Fortune 100 companies and family-owned businesses with fewer than twenty people. He is famous for his deep belly laughs and eating copious amounts of Ozzie rolls. He lives with his wife Tracy and their family in Green Bay, Wisconsin.

DR. PAUL METLER is vice president of Content Development at InitiativeOne, Institute of Business Leadership. His experience is a mosaic of leading and serving. He developed his leadership skills early in life while working with his father and brother in their family-owned trucking business. He then gained more than twenty-five years of experience as a pastor.

Under the leadership of Dr. Fred Johnson, Dr. Metler began capturing the InitiativeOne content in writing and working with executive teams worldwide. An expert in organizational leadership, he is a recognized author, speaker, and professor who has engaged with leaders in North and South America as well as Asia. He lives in Knoxville, Tennessee, with his wife Lynn and son Nick.

ACKNOWLEDGMENTS

To the InitiativeOne Team. Thank you to Tim Felmer, Kabeer Gbaja-Biamila, Lisa Harmann, John Hemken, and Melissa Lacroix for daily inspiration.

Thanks to the outstanding professionals at 9th Street Publishing.
Thank you Joe Kiedinger, Lori O'Connor, Emily Katers, and Kristen Kutil.

To our editor, Barbara McNichol, who makes our writing better.

To Graham Van Dixhorn for his creative contribution to our cover text.

To Fred's wife, Tracy Johnson, who offers unconditional support each and every day, both professionally and personally. There is no greater gift.

To Paul's wife, Lynn Metler and son, Nick, who offer consistent love and support.

Most of all, to God, our ultimate source of transformation.

THE REALITY OF CHANGE

COMING SOON!
BOOK THREE

RISING TIDE LEADERSHIP SERIES

THE REALITY OF CHANGE